The History of

Volume 1: An Introduction

Other books by Michel Foucault available in Vintage:

The History of Sexuality

Volume I: An Introduction

by Michel Foucault

*Translated from the French
by Robert Hurley*

Vintage Books
A Division of Random House
New York

FIRST VINTAGE BOOKS EDITION, January 1980

English translation Copyright © 1978 by Random House, Inc.
All rights reserved under International and Pan-American Copyright Conventions. Published in the United States by Random House, Inc., New York, and in Canada by Random House of Canada Limited, Toronto. Originally published in France as *La Volenté de savoir* by Editions Gallimard, Paris. Copyright © 1976 by Editions Gallimard. First American edition published by Pantheon Books, a division of Random House, Inc., in November, 1978.

Grateful acknowledgment is made to Doubleday & Company, Inc., for permission to reprint an excerpt from a poem by Gottfried August Bürger cited by Arthur Schopenhauer in *The Metaphysics of the Love of the Sexes,* from *The Will to Live: Selected Writings of Arthur Schopenhauer,* edited by Richard Taylor.

Library of Congress Cataloging in Publication Data
Foucault, Michel.
   The history of sexuality.
   Translation of Histoire de la sexualité.
   CONTENTS: v. 1. An introduction.
   1. Sex customs—History—Collected works. I. Title.
HQ12.F6813 1980   301.41'7   79-7460
ISBN 0-394-74026-2

Manufactured in the United States of America
Cover photo courtesy of The Bettmann Archive, Inc.

Contents

PART ONE

We "Other Victorians"

For a long time, the story goes, we supported a Victorian regime, and we continue to be dominated by it even today. Thus the image of the imperial prude is emblazoned on our restrained, mute, and hypocritical sexuality.

At the beginning of the seventeenth century a certain frankness was still common, it would seem. Sexual practices had little need of secrecy; words were said without undue reticence, and things were done without too much conceal- ment; one had a tolerant familiarity with the illicit. Codes regulating the coarse, the obscene, and the indecent were quite lax compared to those of the nineteenth century. It was a time of direct gestures, shameless discourse, and open transgressions, when anatomies were shown and intermin- gled at will, and knowing children hung about amid the laughter of adults: it was a period when bodies "made a display of themselves."

But twilight soon fell upon this bright day, followed by the monotonous nights of the Victorian bourgeoisie. Sexuality was carefully confined; it moved into the home. The conjugal family took custody of it and absorbed it into the serious function of reproduction. On the subject of sex, silence be- came the rule. The legitimate and procreative couple laid down the law. The couple imposed itself as model, enforced the norm, safeguarded the truth, and reserved the right to speak while retaining the principle of secrecy. A single locus of sexuality was acknowledged in social space as well as at the heart of every household, but it was a utilitarian and fertile one: the parents' bedroom. The rest had only to re- main vague; proper demeanor avoided contact with other bodies, and verbal decency sanitized one's speech. And ster-

3

ile behavior carried the taint of abnormality; if it insisted on making itself too visible, it would be designated accordingly and would have to pay the penalty.

Nothing that was not ordered in terms of generation or transfigured by it could expect sanction or protection. Nor did it merit a hearing. It would be driven out, denied, and reduced to silence. Not only did it not exist, it had no right to exist and would be made to disappear upon its least manifestation—whether in acts or in words. Everyone knew, for example, that children had no sex, which was why they were forbidden to talk about it, why one closed one's eyes and stopped one's ears whenever they came to show evidence to the contrary, and why a general and studied silence was imposed. These are the characteristic features attributed to repression, which serve to distinguish it from the prohibitions maintained by penal law: repression operated as a sentence to disappear, but also as an injunction to silence, an affirmation of nonexistence, and, by implication, an admission that there was nothing to say about such things, nothing to see, and nothing to know. Such was the hypocrisy of our bourgeois societies with its halting logic. It was forced to make a few concessions, however. If it was truly necessary to make room for illegitimate sexualities, it was reasoned, let them take their infernal mischief elsewhere: to a place where they could be reintegrated, if not in the circuits of production, at least in those of profit. The brothel and the mental hospital would be those places of tolerance: the prostitute, the client, and the pimp, together with the psychiatrist and his hysteric—those "other Victorians," as Steven Marcus would say—seem to have surreptitiously transferred the pleasures that are unspoken into the order of things that are counted. Words and gestures, quietly authorized, could be exchanged there at the going rate. Only in those places would untrammeled sex have a right to (safely insularized) forms of reality, and only to clandestine, circumscribed, and coded types of discourse. Everywhere else, modern puritanism imposed its triple edict of taboo, nonexistence, and silence.

But have we not liberated ourselves from those two long centuries in which the history of sexuality must be seen first of all as the chronicle of an increasing repression? Only to a slight extent, we are told. Perhaps some progress was made by Freud; but with such circumspection, such medical prudence, a scientific guarantee of innocuousness, and so many precautions in order to contain everything, with no fear of "overflow," in that safest and most discrete of spaces, between the couch and discourse: yet another round of whispering on a bed. And could things have been otherwise? We are informed that if repression has indeed been the fundamental link between power, knowledge, and sexuality since the classical age, it stands to reason that we will not be able to free ourselves from it except at a considerable cost: nothing less than a transgression of laws, a lifting of prohibitions, an irruption of speech, a reinstating of pleasure within reality, and a whole new economy in the mechanisms of power will be required. For the least glimmer of truth is conditioned by politics. Hence, one cannot hope to obtain the desired results simply from a medical practice, nor from a theoretical discourse, however rigorously pursued. Thus, one denounces Freud's conformism, the normalizing functions of psychoanalysis, the obvious timidity underlying Reich's vehemence, and all the effects of integration ensured by the "science" of sex and the barely equivocal practices of sexology.

This discourse on modern sexual repression holds up well, owing no doubt to how easy it is to uphold. A solemn historical and political guarantee protects it. By placing the advent of the age of repression in the seventeenth century, after hundreds of years of open spaces and free expression, one adjusts it to coincide with the development of capitalism: it becomes an integral part of the bourgeois order. The minor chronicle of sex and its trials is transposed into the ceremonious history of the modes of production; its trifling aspect fades from view. A principle of explanation emerges after the fact: if sex is so rigorously repressed, this is because it is incompatible with a general and intensive work imperative. At a time when labor capacity was being systematically exploited, how could this capacity be allowed to dissipate itself in pleasurable pursuits, except in those—reduced to a minimum—that enabled it to reproduce itself? Sex and its effects are perhaps not so easily deciphered; on the other hand, their repression, thus reconstructed, is easily analyzed. And the sexual cause—the demand for sexual freedom, but also for the knowledge to be gained from sex and the right to speak about it—becomes legitimately associated with the honor of a political cause: sex too is placed on the agenda for the future. A suspicious mind might wonder if taking so many precautions in order to give the history of sex such an impressive filiation does not bear traces of the same old prudishness: as if those valorizing correlations were necessary before such a discourse could be formulated or accepted.

But there may be another reason that makes it so gratifying for us to define the relationship between sex and power in terms of repression: something that one might call the speaker's benefit. If sex is repressed, that is, condemned to prohibition, nonexistence, and silence, then the mere fact that one is speaking about it has the appearance of a deliberate transgression. A person who holds forth in such language places himself to a certain extent outside the reach of power; he upsets established law; he somehow anticipates the coming freedom. This explains the solemnity with which one speaks of sex nowadays. When they had to allude to it, the first demographers and psychiatrists of the nineteenth century thought it advisable to excuse themselves for asking their readers to dwell on matters so trivial and base. But for decades now, we have found it difficult to speak on the subject without striking a different pose: we are conscious of defying established power, our tone of voice shows that we know we are being subversive, and we ardently conjure away the present and appeal to the future, whose day will be hastened by the contribution we believe we are making. Something that smacks of revolt, of promised freedom, of the coming age of a different law, slips easily into this discourse on sexual oppression. Some of the ancient functions of prophecy are reactivated therein. Tomorrow sex will be good again. Because this repression is affirmed, one can discreetly bring into coexistence concepts which the fear of ridicule or the bitterness of history prevents most of us from putting side by side: revolution and happiness; or revolution and a different body, one that is newer and more beautiful; or indeed, revolution and pleasure. What sustains our eagerness to speak of sex in terms of repression is doubtless this opportunity to speak out against the powers that be, to utter truths and promise bliss, to link together enlightenment, liberation, and manifold pleasures; to pronounce a discourse that combines the fervor of knowledge, the determination to change the laws, and the longing for the garden of earthly delights. This is perhaps what also explains the market value attributed not only to what is said about sexual repression, but also to the mere fact of lending an ear to those who would eliminate the effects of repression. Ours is, after all, the only civilization in which officials are paid to listen to all and sundry impart the secrets of their sex: as if the urge to talk about it, and the interest one hopes to arouse by doing so, have far surpassed the possibilities of being heard, so that some individuals have even offered their ears for hire.

But it appears to me that the essential thing is not this economic factor, but rather the existence in our era of a discourse in which sex, the revelation of truth, the overturning of global laws, the proclamation of a new day to come, and the promise of a certain felicity are linked together. Today it is sex that serves as a support for the ancient form —so familiar and important in the West—of preaching. A great sexual sermon—which has had its subtle theologians and its popular voices—has swept through our societies over the last decades; it has chastised the old order, denounced hypocrisy, and praised the rights of the immediate and the real; it has made people dream of a New City. The Franciscans are called to mind. And we might wonder how it is possible that the lyricism and religiosity that long accompanied the revolutionary project have, in Western industrial societies, been largely carried over to sex.

The notion of repressed sex is not, therefore, only a theoretical matter. The affirmation of a sexuality that has never been more rigorously subjugated than during the age of the hypocritical, bustling, and responsible bourgeoisie is coupled with the grandiloquence of a discourse purporting to reveal the truth about sex, modify its economy within reality, subvert the law that governs it, and change its future. The statement of oppression and the form of the sermon refer back to one another; they are mutually reinforcing. To say that sex is not repressed, or rather that the relationship between sex and power is not characterized by repression, is to risk falling into a sterile paradox. It not only runs counter to a well-accepted argument, it goes against the whole economy and all the discursive "interests" that underlie this argument.

This is the point at which I would like to situate the series of historical analyses that will follow, the present volume being at the same time an introduction and a first attempt at an overview: it surveys a few historically significant points and outlines certain theoretical problems. Briefly, my aim is to examine the case of a society which has been loudly castigating itself for its hypocrisy for more than a century, which speaks verbosely of its own silence, takes great pains to relate in detail the things it does not say, denounces the powers it exercises, and promises to liberate itself from the very laws that have made it function. I would like to explore not only these discourses but also the will that sustains them and the strategic intention that supports them. The question I would like to pose is not, Why are we repressed? but rather, Why do we say, with so much passion and so much resentment against our most recent past, against our present, and against ourselves, that we are repressed? By what spiral did we come to affirm that sex is negated? What led us to show, ostentatiously, that sex is something we hide, to say it is something we silence? And we do all this by formulating the matter in the most explicit terms, by trying to reveal it in its most naked reality, by affirming it in the positivity of its power and its effects. It is certainly legitimate to ask why sex was associated with sin for such a long time—although it would remain to be discovered how this association was formed, and one would have to be careful not to state in a summary and hasty fashion that sex was "condemned"—but we must also ask why we burden ourselves today with so much guilt for having once made sex a sin. What paths have brought us to the point where we are "at fault" with respect to our own sex? And how have we come to be a civilization so peculiar as to tell itself that, through an abuse of power which has not ended, it has long "sinned" against sex? How does one account for the displacement which, while claiming to free us from the sinful nature of sex, taxes us with a great historical wrong which consists precisely in imagining that nature to be blameworthy and in drawing disastrous consequences from that belief?

It will be said that if so many people today affirm this repression, the reason is that it is historically evident. And if they speak of it so abundantly, as they have for such a long time now, this is because repression is so firmly anchored, having solid roots and reasons, and weighs so heavily on sex that more than one denunciation will be required in order to free ourselves from it; the job will be a long one. All the longer, no doubt, as it is in the nature of power—particularly the kind of power that operates in our society—to be repressive, and to be especially careful in repressing useless energies, the intensity of pleasures, and irregular modes of behavior. We must not be surprised, then, if the effects of liberation vis-à-vis this repressive power are so slow to manifest themselves; the effort to speak freely about sex and accept it in its reality is so alien to a historical sequence that has gone unbroken for a thousand years now, and so inimical to the intrinsic mechanisms of power, that it is bound to make little headway for a long time before succeeding in its mission.

One can raise three serious doubts concerning what I shall term the "repressive hypothesis." First doubt: Is sexual repression truly an established historical fact? Is what first comes into view—and consequently permits one to advance an initial hypothesis—really the accentuation or even the establishment of a regime of sexual repression beginning in the seventeenth century? This is a properly historical question. Second doubt: Do the workings of power, and in particular those mechanisms that are brought into play in societies such as ours, really belong primarily to the category of repression? Are prohibition, censorship, and denial truly the forms through which power is exercised in a general way, if not in every society, most certainly in our own? This is a historico-theoretical question. A third and final doubt: Did the critical discourse that addresses itself to repression come to act as a roadblock to a power mechanism that had operated unchallenged up to that point, or is it not in fact part of the same historical network as the thing it denounces (and doubtless misrepresents) by calling it "repression"? Was there really a historical rupture between the age of repression and the critical analysis of repression? This is a historico-political question. My purpose in introducing these three doubts is not merely to construct counterarguments that are symmetrical and contrary to those outlined above; it is not a matter of saying that sexuality, far from being repressed in capitalist and bourgeois societies, has on the contrary benefitted from a regime of unchanging liberty; nor is it a matter of saying that power in societies such as ours is more tolerant than repressive, and that the critique of repression, while it may give itself airs of a rupture with the past, actually forms part of a much older process and, depending on how one chooses to understand this process, will appear either as a new episode in the lessening of prohibitions, or as a more devious and discreet form of power.

The doubts I would like to oppose to the repressive hypothesis are aimed less at showing it to be mistaken than at putting it back within a general economy of discourses on sex in modern societies since the seventeenth century. Why has sexuality been so widely discussed, and what has been said about it? What were the effects of power generated by what was said? What are the links between these discourses, these effects of power, and the pleasures that were invested by them? What knowledge (savoir) was formed as a result of this linkage? The object, in short, is to define the regime of power-knowledge-pleasure that sustains the discourse on human sexuality in our part of the world. The central issue, then (at least in the first instance), is not to determine whether one says yes or no to sex, whether one formulates prohibitions or permissions, whether one asserts its importance or denies its effects, or whether one refines the words one uses to designate it; but to account for the fact that it is spoken about, to discover who does the speaking, the positions and viewpoints from which they speak, the institutions which prompt people to speak about it and which store and distribute the things that are said. What is at issue, briefly, is the over-all "discursive fact," the way in which sex is "put into discourse." Hence, too, my main concern will be to locate the forms of power, the channels it takes, and the discourses it permeates in order to reach the most tenuous and individual modes of behavior, the paths that give it access to the rare or scarcely perceivable forms of desire, how it penetrates and controls everyday pleasure—all this entailing effects that may be those of refusal, blockage, and invalidation, but also incitement and intensification: in short, the "polymorphous techniques of power." And finally, the essential aim will not be to determine whether these discursive productions and these effects of power lead one to formulate the truth about sex, or on the contrary falsehoods designed to conceal that truth, but rather to bring out the "will to knowledge" that serves as both their support and their instrument.

Let there be no misunderstanding: I do not claim that sex has not been prohibited or barred or masked or misapprehended since the classical age; nor do I even assert that it has suffered these things any less from that period on than before. I do not maintain that the prohibition of sex is a ruse; but it is a ruse to make prohibition into the basic and constitutive element from which one would be able to write the history of what has been said concerning sex starting from the modern epoch. All these negative elements—defenses, censorships, denials—which the repressive hypothesis groups together in one great central mechanism destined to say no, are doubtless only component parts that have a local and tactical role to play in a transformation into discourse, a technology of power, and a will to knowledge that are far from being reducible to the former.

In short, I would like to disengage my analysis from the privileges generally accorded the economy of scarcity and the principles of rarefaction, to search instead for instances of discursive production (which also administer silences, to be sure), of the production of power (which sometimes have the function of prohibiting), of the propagation of knowledge (which often cause mistaken beliefs or systematic misconceptions to circulate); I would like to write the history of these instances and their transformations. A first survey made from this viewpoint seems to indicate that since the end of the sixteenth century, the "putting into discourse of sex," far from undergoing a process of restriction, on the contrary has been subjected to a mechanism of increasing incitement; that the techniques of power exercised over sex have not obeyed a principle of rigorous selection, but rather one of dissemination and implantation of polymorphous sexualities; and that the will to knowledge has not come to a halt in the face of a taboo that must not be lifted, but has persisted in constituting—despite many mistakes, of course—a science of sexuality. It is these movements that I will now attempt to bring into focus in a schematic way, bypassing as it were the repressive hypothesis and the facts of interdiction or exclusion it invokes, and starting from certain historical facts that serve as guidelines for research.

PART TWO

The Repressive
Hypothesis

I

The Incitement
to Discourse

The seventeenth century, then, was the beginning of an age of repression emblematic of what we call the bourgeois societies, an age which perhaps we still have not completely left behind. Calling sex by its name thereafter became more difficult and more costly. As if in order to gain mastery over it in reality, it had first been necessary to subjugate it at the level of language, control its free circulation in speech, expunge it from the things that were said, and extinguish the words that rendered it too visibly present. And even these prohibitions, it seems, were afraid to name it. Without even having to pronounce the word, modern prudishness was able to ensure that one did not speak of sex, merely through the interplay of prohibitions that referred back to one another: instances of muteness which, by dint of saying nothing, imposed silence. Censorship.

Yet when one looks back over these last three centuries with their continual transformations, things appear in a very different light: around and apropos of sex, one sees a veritable discursive explosion. We must be clear on this point, however. It is quite possible that there was an expurgation—and a very rigorous one—of the authorized vocabulary. It may indeed be true that a whole rhetoric of allusion and metaphor was codified. Without question, new rules of propriety screened out some words: there was a policing of statements. A control over enunciations as well: where and when it was not possible to talk about such things became much more strictly defined; in which circumstances, among which speakers, and within which social relationships. Areas were thus established, if not of utter silence, at least of tact and discretion: between parents and children, for instance, or teachers and pupils, or masters and domestic servants. This almost certainly constituted a whole restrictive economy, one that was incorporated into that politics of language and speech—spontaneous on the one hand, concerted on the other—which accompanied the social redistributions of the classical period.

At the level of discourses and their domains, however, practically the opposite phenomenon occurred. There was a steady proliferation of discourses concerned with sex—specific discourses, different from one another both by their form and by their object: a discursive ferment that gathered momentum from the eighteenth century onward. Here I am thinking not so much of the probable increase in "illicit" discourses, that is, discourses of infraction that crudely named sex by way of insult or mockery of the new code of decency; the tightening up of the rules of decorum likely did produce, as a countereffect, a valorization and intensification of indecent speech. But more important was the multiplication of discourses concerning sex in the field of exercise of power itself: an institutional incitement to speak about it, and to do so more and more; a determination on the part of the agencies of power to hear it spoken about, and to cause *it* to speak through explicit articulation and endlessly accumulated detail.

Consider the evolution of the Catholic pastoral and the sacrament of penance after the Council of Trent. Little by little, the nakedness of the questions formulated by the confession manuals of the Middle Ages, and a good number of those still in use in the seventeenth century, was veiled. One avoided entering into that degree of detail which some authors, such as Sanchez or Tamburini, had for a long time believed indispensable for the confession to be complete: description of the respective positions of the partners, the postures assumed, gestures, places touched, caresses, the precise moment of pleasure—an entire painstaking review of the sexual act in its very unfolding. Discretion was advised, with increasing emphasis. The greatest reserve was counseled when dealing with sins against purity: "This matter is similar to pitch, for, however one might handle it, even to cast it far from oneself, it sticks nonetheless, and always soils."[1] And later, Alfonso de' Liguori prescribed starting—and possibly going no further, especially when dealing with children—with questions that were "roundabout and vague."[2]

But while the language may have been refined, the scope of the confession—the confession of the flesh—continually increased. This was partly because the Counter Reformation busied itself with stepping up the rhythm of the yearly confession in the Catholic countries, and because it tried to impose meticulous rules of self-examination; but above all, because it attributed more and more importance in penance —and perhaps at the expense of some other sins—to all the insinuations of the flesh: thoughts, desires, voluptuous imaginings, delectations, combined movements of the body and the soul; henceforth all this had to enter, in detail, into the process of confession and guidance. According to the new pastoral, sex must not be named imprudently, but its aspects, its correlations, and its effects must be pursued down to their slenderest ramifications: a shadow in a daydream, an image too slowly dispelled, a badly exorcised complicity between the body's mechanics and the mind's complacency: everything had to be told. A twofold evolution tended to make the flesh into the root of all evil, shifting the most important moment of transgression from the act itself to the stirrings

[1] Paolo Segneri, *L'Instruction du pénitent* (French trans. 1695), p. 301.
[2] Alfonso de' Liguori, *Pratique des confesseurs* (French trans. 1854), p. 140.

—so difficult to perceive and formulate—of desire. For this was an evil that afflicted the whole man, and in the most secret of forms: "Examine diligently, therefore, all the faculties of your soul: memory, understanding, and will. Examine with precision all your senses as well. . . . Examine, moreover, all your thoughts, every word you speak, and all your actions. Examine even unto your dreams, to know if, once awakened, you did not give them your consent. And finally, do not think that in so sensitive and perilous a matter as this, there is anything trivial or insignificant."[3] Discourse, therefore, had to trace the meeting line of the body and the soul, following all its meanderings: beneath the surface of the sins, it would lay bare the unbroken nervure of the flesh. Under the authority of a language that had been carefully expurgated so that it was no longer directly named, sex was taken charge of, tracked down as it were, by a discourse that aimed to allow it no obscurity, no respite.

It was here, perhaps, that the injunction, so peculiar to the West, was laid down for the first time, in the form of a general constraint. I am not talking about the obligation to admit to violations of the laws of sex, as required by traditional penance; but of the nearly infinite task of telling—telling oneself and another, as often as possible, everything that might concern the interplay of innumerable pleasures, sensations, and thoughts which, through the body and the soul, had some affinity with sex. This scheme for transforming sex into discourse had been devised long before in an ascetic and monastic setting. The seventeenth century made it into a rule for everyone. It would seem in actual fact that it could scarcely have applied to any but a tiny elite; the great majority of the faithful who only went to confession on rare occasions in the course of the year escaped such complex prescriptions. But the important point no doubt is that this obligation was decreed, as an ideal at least, for every good

[3]Segneri, *L'Instruction du pénitent*, pp. 301–2.

Christian. An imperative was established: Not only will you confess to acts contravening the law, but you will seek to transform your desire, your every desire, into discourse. Insofar as possible, nothing was meant to elude this dictum, even if the words it employed had to be carefully neutralized. The Christian pastoral prescribed as a fundamental duty the task of passing everything having to do with sex through the endless mill of speech.[4] The forbidding of certain words, the decency of expressions, all the censorings of vocabulary, might well have been only secondary devices compared to that great subjugation: ways of rendering it morally acceptable and technically useful.

One could plot a line going straight from the seventeenth-century pastoral to what became its projection in literature, "scandalous" literature at that. "Tell everything," the directors would say time and again: "not only consummated acts, but sensual touchings, all impure gazes, all obscene remarks . . . all consenting thoughts."[5] Sade takes up the injunction in words that seem to have been retranscribed from the treatises of spirtual direction: "Your narrations must be decorated with the most numerous and searching details; the precise way and extent to which we may judge how the passion you describe relates to human manners and man's character is determined by your willingness to disguise no circumstance; and what is more, the least circumstance is apt to have an immense influence upon the procuring of that kind of sensory irritation we expect from your stories."[6] And again at the end of the nineteenth century, the anonymous author of *My Secret Life* submitted to the same prescription; outwardly, at least, this man was doubtless a kind of tradi-

[4]The reformed pastoral also laid down rules, albeit in a more discreet way, for putting sex into discourse. This notion will be developed in the next volume, *The Body and the Flesh*.

[5]Alfonso de' Liguori, *Préceptes sur le sixième commandement* (French trans. 1835), p. 5.

[6]Donatien-Alphonse de Sade, *The 120 Days of Sodom*, trans. Austryn Wainhouse and Richard Seaver (New York: Grove Press, 1966), p. 271.

tional libertine; but he conceived the idea of complementing his life—which he had almost totally dedicated to sexual activity—with a scrupulous account of every one of its episodes. He sometimes excuses himself by stressing his concern to educate young people, this man who had eleven volumes published, in a printing of only a few copies, which were devoted to the least adventures, pleasures, and sensations of his sex. It is best to take him at his word when he lets into his text the voice of a pure imperative: "I recount the facts, just as they happened, insofar as I am able to recollect them; this is all that I can do"; "a secret life must not leave out anything; there is nothing to be ashamed of . . . one can never know too much concerning human nature."[7] The solitary author of *My Secret Life* often says, in order to justify his describing them, that his strangest practices undoubtedly were shared by thousands of men on the surface of the earth. But the guiding principle for the strangest of these practices, which was the fact of recounting them all, and in detail, from day to day, had been lodged in the heart of modern man for over two centuries. Rather than seeing in this singular man a courageous fugitive from a "Victorianism" that would have compelled him to silence, I am inclined to think that, in an epoch dominated by (highly prolix) directives enjoining discretion and modesty, he was the most direct and in a way the most naïve representative of a plurisecular injunction to talk about sex. The historical accident would consist rather of the reticences of "Victorian puritanism"; at any rate, they were a digression, a refinement, a tactical diversion in the great process of transforming sex into discourse.

This nameless Englishman will serve better than his queen as the central figure for a sexuality whose main features were already taking shape with the Christian pastoral. Doubtless, in contrast to the latter, for him it was a matter of augmenting the sensations he experienced with the details of what he

[7] Anonymous, *My Secret Life,* (New York: Grove Press, 1966).

said about them; like Sade, he wrote "for his pleasure alone," in the strongest sense of the expression; he carefully mixed the editing and rereading of his text with erotic scenes which those writer's activities repeated, prolonged, and stimulated. But after all, the Christian pastoral also sought to produce specific effects on desire, by the mere fact of transforming it —fully and deliberately—into discourse: effects of mastery and detachment, to be sure, but also an effect of spiritual reconversion, of turning back to God, a physical effect of blissful suffering from feeling in one's body the pangs of temptation and the love that resists it. This is the essential thing: that Western man has been drawn for three centuries to the task of telling everything concerning his sex; that since the classical age there has been a constant optimization and an increasing valorization of the discourse on sex; and that this carefully analytical discourse was meant to yield multiple effects of displacement, intensification, reorientation, and modification of desire itself. Not only were the boundaries of what one could say about sex enlarged, and men compelled to hear it said; but more important, discourse was connected to sex by a complex organization with varying effects, by a deployment that cannot be adequately explained merely by referring it to a law of prohibition. A censorship of sex? There was installed rather an apparatus for producing an ever greater quantity of discourse about sex, capable of functioning and taking effect in its very economy.

This technique might have remained tied to the destiny of Christian spirituality if it had not been supported and relayed by other mechanisms. In the first place, by a "public interest." Not a collective curiosity or sensibility; not a new mentality; but power mechanisms that functioned in such a way that discourse on sex—for reasons that will have to be examined—became essential. Toward the beginning of the eighteenth century, there emerged a political, economic, and technical incitement to talk about sex. And not so much in the form of a general theory of sexuality as in the form of analysis, stocktaking, classification, and specification, of quantitative or causal studies. This need to take sex "into account," to pronounce a discourse on sex that would not derive from morality alone but from rationality as well, was sufficiently new that at first it wondered at itself and sought apologies for its own existence. How could a discourse based on reason speak of *that?* "Rarely have philosophers directed a steady gaze to these objects situated between disgust and ridicule, where one must avoid both hypocrisy and scandal."[8] And nearly a century later, the medical establishment, which one might have expected to be less surprised by what it was about to formulate, still stumbled at the moment of speaking: "The darkness that envelops these facts, the shame and disgust they inspire, have always repelled the observer's gaze. . . . For a long time I hesitated to introduce the loathsome picture into this study."[9] What is essential is not in all these scruples, in the "moralism" they betray, or in the hypocrisy one can suspect them of, but in the recognized necessity of overcoming this hesitation. One had to speak of sex; one had to speak publicly and in a manner that was not determined by the division between licit and illicit, even if the speaker maintained the distinction for himself (which is what these solemn and preliminary declarations were intended to show): one had to speak of it as of a thing to be not simply condemned or tolerated but managed, inserted into systems of utility, regulated for the greater good of all, made to function according to an optimum. Sex was not something one simply judged; it was a thing one administered. It was in the nature of a public potential; it called for management procedures; it had to be taken charge of by analytical discourses. In the eighteenth century, sex became a "police" matter—in the full and strict sense given the term at the time: not the repression of disorder, but an ordered maximization

[8]Condorcet, cited by Jean-Louis Flandrin, *Familles: parenté, maison, sexualité dans l'ancienne société,* (Paris: Hachette, 1976).
[9]Auguste Tardieu, *Étude médico-légale sur les attentats aux moeurs* (1857), p. 114.

of collective and individual forces: "We must consolidate and augment, through the wisdom of its regulations, the internal power of the state; and since this power consists not only in the Republic in general, and in each of the members who constitute it, but also in the faculties and talents of those belonging to it, it follows that the police must concern themselves with these means and make them serve the public welfare. And they can only obtain this result through the knowledge they have of those different assets."[10] A policing of sex: that is, not the rigor of a taboo, but the necessity of regulating sex through useful and public discourses.

A few examples will suffice. One of the great innovations in the techniques of power in the eighteenth century was the emergence of "population" as an economic and political problem: population as wealth, population as manpower or labor capacity, population balanced between its own growth and the resources it commanded. Governments perceived that they were not dealing simply with subjects, or even with a "people," but with a "population," with its specific phenomena and its peculiar variables: birth and death rates, life expectancy, fertility, state of health, frequency of illnesses, patterns of diet and habitation. All these variables were situated at the point where the characteristic movements of life and the specific effects of institutions intersected: "States are not populated in accordance with the natural progression of propagation, but by virtue of their industry, their products, and their different institutions. . . . Men multiply like the yields from the ground and in proportion to the advantages and resources they find in their labors."[11] At the heart of this economic and political problem of population was sex: it was necessary to analyze the birthrate, the age of marriage, the legitimate and illegitimate births, the precocity and frequency of sexual relations, the ways of making them fertile or sterile, the effects of unmar-

[10]Johann von Justi, *Éléments généraux de police* (French trans. 1769), p. 20.
[11]Claude-Jacques Herbert, *Essai sur la police générale des grains* (1753), pp. 320–1.

ried life or of the prohibitions, the impact of contraceptive practices—of those notorious "deadly secrets" which demographers on the eve of the Revolution knew were already familiar to the inhabitants of the countryside.

Of course, it had long been asserted that a country had to be populated if it hoped to be rich and powerful; but this was the first time that a society had affirmed, in a constant way, that its future and its fortune were tied not only to the number and the uprightness of its citizens, to their marriage rules and family organization, but to the manner in which each individual made use of his sex. Things went from ritual lamenting over the unfruitful debauchery of the rich, bachelors, and libertines to a discourse in which the sexual conduct of the population was taken both as an object of analysis and as a target of intervention; there was a progression from the crudely populationist arguments of the mercantilist epoch to the much more subtle and calculated attempts at regulation that tended to favor or discourage—according to the objectives and exigencies of the moment—an increasing birthrate. Through the political economy of population there was formed a whole grid of observations regarding sex. There emerged the analysis of the modes of sexual conduct, their determinations and their effects, at the boundary line of the biological and the economic domains. There also appeared those systematic campaigns which, going beyond the traditional means—moral and religious exhortations, fiscal measures—tried to transform the sexual conduct of couples into a concerted economic and political behavior. In time these new measures would become anchorage points for the different varieties of racism of the nineteenth and twentieth centuries. It was essential that the state know what was happening with its citizens' sex, and the use they made of it, but also that each individual be capable of controlling the use he made of it. Between the state and the individual, sex became an issue, and a public issue no less; a whole web of discourses, special knowledges, analyses, and injunctions settled upon it.

The situation was similar in the case of children's sex. It is often said that the classical period consigned it to an obscurity from which it scarcely emerged before the *Three Essays* or the beneficent anxieties of Little Hans. It is true that a longstanding "freedom" of language between children and adults, or pupils and teachers, may have disappeared. No seventeenth-century pedagogue would have publicly advised his disciple, as did Erasmus in his *Dialogues,* on the choice of a good prostitute. And the boisterous laughter that had accompanied the precocious sexuality of children for so long—and in all social classes, it seems—was gradually stifled. But this was not a plain and simple imposition of silence. Rather, it was a new regime of discourses. Not any less was said about it; on the contrary. But things were said in a different way; it was different people who said them, from different points of view, and in order to obtain different results. Silence itself—the things one declines to say, or is forbidden to name, the discretion that is required between different speakers—is less the absolute limit of discourse, the other side from which it is separated by a strict boundary, than an element that functions alongside the things said, with them and in relation to them within over-all strategies. There is no binary division to be made between what one says and what one does not say; we must try to determine the different ways of not saying such things, how those who can and those who cannot speak of them are distributed, which type of discourse is authorized, or which form of discretion is required in either case. There is not one but many silences, and they are an integral part of the strategies that underlie and permeate discourses.

Take the secondary schools of the eighteenth century, for example. On the whole, one can have the impression that sex was hardly spoken of at all in these institutions. But one only has to glance over the architectural layout, the rules of discipline, and their whole internal organization: the question of sex was a constant preoccupation. The builders considered it explicitly. The organizers took it permanently into account. All who held a measure of authority were placed in a state of perpetual alert, which the fixtures, the precautions taken, the interplay of punishments and responsibilities, never ceased to reiterate. The space for classes, the shape of the tables, the planning of the recreation lessons, the distribution of the dormitories (with or without partitions, with or without curtains), the rules for monitoring bedtime and sleep periods—all this referred, in the most prolix manner, to the sexuality of children.[12] What one might call the internal discourse of the institution—the one it employed to address itself, and which circulated among those who made it function—was largely based on the assumption that this sexuality existed, that it was precocious, active, and ever present. But this was not all: the sex of the schoolboy became in the course of the eighteenth century—and quite apart from that of adolescents in general—a public problem. Doctors counseled the directors and professors of educational establishments, but they also gave their opinions to families; educators designed projects which they submitted to the authorities; schoolmasters turned to students, made recommendations to them, and drafted for their benefit books of exhortation, full of moral and medical examples. Around the schoolboy and his sex there proliferated a whole literature of precepts, opinions, observations, medical advice, clinical cases, outlines for reform, and plans for ideal institutions. With Basedow and the German "philanthropic" movement, this transformation of adolescent sex into discourse grew to considerable dimensions. Salzmann even organized an experimental school

[12]*Règlement de police pour les lycées* (1809), art. 67: "There shall always be, during class and study hours, an instructor watching the exterior, so as to prevent students who have gone out to relieve themselves from stopping and congregating.

art. 68: "After the evening prayer, the students will be conducted back to the dormitory, where the schoolmasters will put them to bed at once.

art. 69: "The masters will not retire except after having made certain that every student is in bed.

art. 70: "The beds shall be separated by partitions two meters in height. The dormitories shall be illuminated during the night."

which owed its exceptional character to a supervision and education of sex so well thought out that youth's universal sin would never need to be practiced there. And with all these measures taken, the child was not to be simply the mute and unconscious object of attentions prearranged between adults only; a certain reasonable, limited, canonical, and truthful discourse on sex was prescribed for him—a kind of discursive orthopedics. The great festival organized at the Philanthropinum in May of 1776 can serve as a vignette in this regard. Taking the form of an examination, mixed with floral games, the awarding of prizes, and a board of review, this was the first solemn communion of adolescent sex and reasonable discourse. In order to show the success of the sex education given the students, Basedow had invited all the dignitaries that Germany could muster (Goethe was one of the few to decline the invitation). Before the assembled public, one of the professors, a certain Wolke, asked the students selected questions concerning the mysteries of sex, birth, and procreation. He had them comment on engravings that depicted a pregnant woman, a couple, and a cradle. The replies were enlightened, offered without shame or embarrassment. No unseemly laughter intervened to disturb them—except from the very ranks of an adult audience more childish than the children themselves, and whom Wolke severely reprimanded. At the end, they all applauded these cherub-faced boys who, in front of adults, had skillfully woven the garlands of discourse and sex.[13]

It would be less than exact to say that the pedagogical institution has imposed a ponderous silence on the sex of children and adolescents. On the contrary, since the eighteenth century it has multiplied the forms of discourse on the subject; it has established various points of implantation for sex; it has coded contents and qualified speakers. Speaking

[13] Johann Gottlieb Schummel, *Fritzens Reise nach Dessau* (1776), cited by Auguste Pinloche, *La Réforme de l'éducation en Allemagne au XVIII⁰ siècle* (1889), pp. 125–9.

about children's sex, inducing educators, physicians, administrators, and parents to speak of it, or speaking to them about it, causing children themselves to talk about it, and enclosing them in a web of discourses which sometimes address them, sometimes speak about them, or impose canonical bits of knowledge on them, or use them as a basis for constructing a science that is beyond their grasp—all this together enables us to link an intensification of the interventions of power to a multiplication of discourse. The sex of children and adolescents has become, since the eighteenth century, an important area of contention around which innumerable institutional devices and discursive strategies have been deployed. It may well be true that adults and children themselves were deprived of a certain way of speaking about sex, a mode that was disallowed as being too direct, crude, or coarse. But this was only the counterpart of other discourses, and perhaps the condition necessary in order for them to function, discourses that were interlocking, hierarchized, and all highly articulated around a cluster of power relations.

One could mention many other centers which in the eighteenth or nineteenth century began to produce discourses on sex. First there was medicine, via the "nervous disorders"; next psychiatry, when it set out to discover the etiology of mental illnesses, focusing its gaze first on "excess," then onanism, then frustration, then "frauds against procreation," but especially when it annexed the whole of the sexual perversions as its own province; criminal justice, too, which had long been concerned with sexuality, particularly in the form of "heinous" crimes and crimes against nature, but which, toward the middle of the nineteenth century, broadened its jurisdiction to include petty offenses, minor indecencies, insignificant perversions; and lastly, all those social controls, cropping up at the end of the last century, which screened the sexuality of couples, parents and children, dangerous and endangered adolescents—undertaking to protect, separate, and forewarn, signaling perils everywhere, awakening people's attention, calling for diagnoses, piling up reports, organizing therapies. These sites radiated discourses aimed at sex, intensifying people's awareness of it as a constant danger, and this in turn created a further incentive to talk about it.

One day in 1867, a farm hand from the village of Lapcourt, who was somewhat simple-minded, employed here then there, depending on the season, living hand-to-mouth from a little charity or in exchange for the worst sort of labor, sleeping in barns and stables, was turned in to the authorities. At the border of a field, he had obtained a few caresses from a little girl, just as he had done before and seen done by the village urchins round about him; for, at the edge of the wood, or in the ditch by the road leading to Saint-Nicolas, they would play the familiar game called "curdled milk." So he was pointed out by the girl's parents to the mayor of the village, reported by the mayor to the gendarmes, led by the gendarmes to the judge, who indicted him and turned him over first to a doctor, then to two other experts who not only wrote their report but also had it published.[14] What is the significant thing about this story? The pettiness of it all; the fact that this everyday occurrence in the life of village sexuality, these inconsequential bucolic pleasures, could become, from a certain time, the object not only of a collective intolerance but of a judicial action, a medical intervention, a careful clinical examination, and an entire theoretical elaboration. The thing to note is that they went so far as to measure the brainpan, study the facial bone structure, and inspect for possible signs of degenerescence the anatomy of this personage who up to that moment had been an integral part of village life; that they made him talk; that they questioned him concerning his thoughts, inclinations, habits, sensations, and opinions. And then, acquitting him of any crime, they

[14] H. Bonnet and J. Bulard, *Rapport médico-légal sur l'état mental de Ch.-J. Jouy,* January 4, 1968.

decided finally to make him into a pure object of medicine and knowledge—an object to be shut away till the end of his life in the hospital at Maréville, but also one to be made known to the world of learning through a detailed analysis. One can be fairly certain that during this same period the Lapcourt schoolmaster was instructing the little villagers to mind their language and not talk about all these things aloud. But this was undoubtedly one of the conditions enabling the institutions of knowledge and power to overlay this everyday bit of theater with their solemn discourse. So it was that our society—and it was doubtless the first in history to take such measures—assembled around these timeless gestures, these barely furtive pleasures between simple-minded adults and alert children, a whole machinery for speechifying, analyzing, and investigating.

Between the licentious Englishman, who earnestly recorded for his own purposes the singular episodes of his secret life, and his contemporary, this village halfwit who would give a few pennies to the little girls for favors the older ones refused him, there was without doubt a profound connection: in any case, from one extreme to the other, sex became something to say, and to say exhaustively in accordance with deployments that were varied, but all, in their own way, compelling. Whether in the form of a subtle confession in confidence or an authoritarian interrogation, sex—be it refined or rustic—had to be put into words. A great polymorphous injunction bound the Englishman and the poor Lorrainese peasant alike. As history would have it, the latter was named Jouy.*

Since the eighteenth century, sex has not ceased to provoke a kind of generalized discursive erethism. And these discourses on sex did not multiply apart from or against power, but in the very space and as the means of its exercise. Incitements to speak were orchestrated from all quarters,

*Jouy sounds like the past participle of *jouir,* the French verb meaning to enjoy, to delight in (something), but also to have an orgasm, to come. (Translator's note)

apparatuses everywhere for listening and recording, procedures for observing, questioning, and formulating. Sex was driven out of hiding and constrained to lead a discursive existence. From the singular imperialism that compels everyone to transform their sexuality into a perpetual discourse, to the manifold mechanisms which, in the areas of economy, pedagogy, medicine, and justice, incite, extract, distribute, and institutionalize the sexual discourse, an immense verbosity is what our civilization has required and organized. Surely no other type of society has ever accumulated—and in such a relatively short span of time—a similar quantity of discourses concerned with sex. It may well be that we talk about sex more than anything else; we set our minds to the task; we convince ourselves that we have never said enough on the subject, that, through inertia or submissiveness, we conceal from ourselves the blinding evidence, and that what is essential always eludes us, so that we must always start out once again in search of it. It is possible that where sex is concerned, the most long-winded, the most impatient of societies is our own.

But as this first overview shows, we are dealing less with *a* discourse on sex than with a multiplicity of discourses produced by a whole series of mechanisms operating in different institutions. The Middle Ages had organized around the theme of the flesh and the practice of penance a discourse that was markedly unitary. In the course of recent centuries, this relative uniformity was broken apart, scattered, and multiplied in an explosion of distinct discursivities which took form in demography, biology, medicine, psychiatry, psychology, ethics, pedagogy, and political criticism. More precisely, the secure bond that held together the moral theology of concupiscence and the obligation of confession (equivalent to the theoretical discourse on sex and its first-person formulation) was, if not broken, at least loosened and diversified: between the objectification of sex in rational discourses, and the movement by which each individual was set to the task of recounting his own sex, there has occurred, since the eighteenth century, a whole series of tensions, conflicts, efforts at adjustment, and attempts at retranscription. So it is not simply in terms of a continual extension that we must speak of this discursive growth; it should be seen rather as a dispersion of centers from which discourses emanated, a diversification of their forms, and the complex deployment of the network connecting them. Rather than the uniform concern to hide sex, rather than a general prudishness of language, what distinguishes these last three centuries is the variety, the wide dispersion of devices that were invented for speaking about it, for having it be spoken about, for inducing it to speak of itself, for listening, recording, transcribing, and redistributing what is said about it: around sex, a whole network of varying, specific, and coercive transpositions into discourse. Rather than a massive censorship, beginning with the verbal proprieties imposed by the Age of Reason, what was involved was a regulated and polymorphous incitement to discourse.

The objection will doubtless be raised that if so many stimulations and constraining mechanisms were necessary in order to speak of sex, this was because there reigned over everyone a certain fundamental prohibition; only definite necessities—economic pressures, political requirements—were able to lift this prohibition and open a few approaches to the discourse on sex, but these were limited and carefully coded; so much talk about sex, so many insistent devices contrived for causing it to be talked about—but under strict conditions: does this not prove that it was an object of secrecy, and more important, that there is still an attempt to keep it that way? But this often-stated theme, that sex is outside of discourse and that only the removing of an obstacle, the breaking of a secret, can clear the way leading to it, is precisely what needs to be examined. Does it not partake of the injunction by which discourse is provoked? Is it not with the aim of inciting people to speak of sex that it is made to mirror, at the outer limit of every actual discourse, something akin to a secret whose discovery is imperative, a thing abusively reduced to silence, and at the same time difficult and necessary, dangerous and precious to divulge? We must not forget that by making sex into that which, above all else, had to be confessed, the Christian pastoral always presented it as the disquieting enigma: not a thing which stubbornly shows itself, but one which always hides, the insidious presence that speaks in a voice so muted and often disguised that one risks remaining deaf to it. Doubtless the secret does not reside in that basic reality in relation to which all the incitements to speak of sex are situated—whether they try to force the secret, or whether in some obscure way they reinforce it by the manner in which they speak of it. It is a question rather of a theme that forms part of the very mechanics of these incitements: a way of giving shape to the requirement to speak about the matter, a fable that is indispensable to the endlessly proliferating economy of the discourse on sex. What is peculiar to modern societies, in fact, is not that they consigned sex to a shadow existence, but that they dedicated themselves to speaking of it *ad infinitum,* while exploiting it as *the* secret.

2

The Perverse Implantation

A possible objection: it would be a mistake to see in this proliferation of discourses merely a quantitative phenomenon, something like a pure increase, as if what was said in them were immaterial, as if the fact of speaking about sex were of itself more important than the forms of imperatives that were imposed on it by speaking about it. For was this transformation of sex into discourse not governed by the endeavor to expel from reality the forms of sexuality that were not amenable to the strict economy of reproduction: to say no to unproductive activities, to banish casual pleasures, to reduce or exclude practices whose object was not procreation? Through the various discourses, legal sanctions against minor perversions were multiplied; sexual irregularity was annexed to mental illness; from childhood to old age, a norm of sexual development was defined and all the possible deviations were carefully described; pedagogical controls and medical treatments were organized; around the least fantasies, moralists, but especially doctors, brandished the whole emphatic vocabulary of abomination. Were these anything more than means employed to absorb, for the benefit of a genitally centered sexuality, all the fruitless pleasures? All this garrulous attention which has us in a stew over sexuality, is it not motivated by one basic concern: to ensure population, to reproduce labor capacity, to perpetuate the form of social relations: in short, to constitute a sexuality that is economically useful and politically conservative?

I still do not know whether this is the ultimate objective. But this much is certain: reduction has not been the means employed for trying to achieve it. The nineteenth century and our own have been rather the age of multiplication: a dispersion of sexualities, a strengthening of their disparate forms, a multiple implantation of "perversions." Our epoch has initiated sexual heterogeneities.

Up to the end of the eighteenth century, three major explicit codes—apart from the customary regularities and constraints of opinion—governed sexual practices: canonical law, the Christian pastoral, and civil law. They determined, each in its own way, the division between licit and illicit. They were all centered on matrimonial relations: the marital obligation, the ability to fulfill it, the manner in which one complied with it, the requirements and violences that accompanied it, the useless or unwarranted caresses for which it was a pretext, its fecundity or the way one went about making it sterile, the moments when one demanded it (dangerous periods of pregnancy or breast-feeding, forbidden times of Lent or abstinence), its frequency or infrequency, and so on. It was this domain that was especially saturated with prescriptions. The sex of husband and wife was beset by rules and recommendations. The marriage relation was the most intense focus of constraints; it was spoken of more than anything else; more than any other relation, it was required to give a detailed accounting of itself. It was under constant surveillance: if it was found to be lacking, it had to come forward and plead its case before a witness. The "rest" remained a good deal more confused: one only has to think of the uncertain status of "sodomy," or the indifference regarding the sexuality of children.

Moreover, these different codes did not make a clear distinction between violations of the rules of marriage and deviations with respect to genitality. Breaking the rules of marriage or seeking strange pleasures brought an equal measure of condemnation. On the list of grave sins, and separated only by their relative importance, there appeared debauchery (extramarital relations), adultery, rape, spiritual or carnal incest, but also sodomy, or the mutual "caress." As to the courts, they could condemn homosexuality as well as infidelity, marriage without parental consent, or bestiality. What was taken into account in the civil and religious jurisdictions alike was a general unlawfulness. Doubtless acts "contrary to nature" were stamped as especially abominable, but they were perceived simply as an extreme form of acts "against the law"; they were infringements of decrees which were just as sacred as those of marriage, and which had been established for governing the order of things and the plan of beings. Prohibitions bearing on sex were essentially of a juridical nature. The "nature" on which they were based was still a kind of law. For a long time hermaphrodites were criminals, or crime's offspring, since their anatomical disposition, their very being, confounded the law that distinguished the sexes and prescribed their union.

The discursive explosion of the eighteenth and nineteenth centuries caused this system centered on legitimate alliance to undergo two modifications. First, a centrifugal movement with respect to heterosexual monogamy. Of course, the array of practices and pleasures continued to be referred to it as their internal standard; but it was spoken of less and less, or in any case with a growing moderation. Efforts to find out its secrets were abandoned; nothing further was demanded of it than to define itself from day to day. The legitimate couple, with its regular sexuality, had a right to more discretion. It tended to function as a norm, one that was stricter, perhaps, but quieter. On the other hand, what came under scrutiny was the sexuality of children, mad men and women, and criminals; the sensuality of those who did not like the opposite sex; reveries, obsessions, petty manias, or great transports of rage. It was time for all these figures, scarcely noticed in the past, to step forward and speak, to make the difficult confession of what they were. No doubt they were condemned all the same; but they were listened to; and if regular sexuality happened to be questioned once again, it was through a reflux movement, originating in these peripheral sexualities.

Whence the setting apart of the "unnatural" as a specific dimension in the field of sexuality. This kind of activity assumed an autonomy with regard to the other condemned forms such as adultery or rape (and the latter were condemned less and less): to marry a close relative or practice sodomy, to seduce a nun or engage in sadism, to deceive one's wife or violate cadavers, became things that were essentially different. The area covered by the Sixth Commandment began to fragment. Similarly, in the civil order, the confused category of "debauchery," which for more than a century had been one of the most frequent reasons for administrative confinement, came apart. From the debris, there appeared on the one hand infractions against the legislation (or morality) pertaining to marriage and the family, and on the other, offenses against the regularity of a natural function (offenses which, it must be added, the law was apt to punish). Here we have a likely reason, among others, for the prestige of Don Juan, which three centuries have not erased. Underneath the great violator of the rules of marriage—stealer of wives, seducer of virgins, the shame of families, and an insult to husbands and fathers—another personage can be glimpsed: the individual driven, in spite of himself, by the somber madness of sex. Underneath the libertine, the pervert. He deliberately breaks the law, but at the same time, something like a nature gone awry transports him far from all nature; his death is the moment when the supernatural return of the crime and its retribution thwarts the flight into counternature. There were two great systems conceived by the West for governing sex: the law of marriage and the order of desires—and the life of Don Juan overturned them both. We shall leave it to psychoanalysts to speculate whether he was homosexual, narcissistic, or impotent.

Although not without delay and equivocation, the natural laws of matrimony and the immanent rules of sexuality began to be recorded on two separate registers. There emerged a world of perversion which partook of that of legal or moral infraction, yet was not simply a variety of the latter. An entire sub-race race was born, different—despite certain kinship ties—from the libertines of the past. From the end of the eighteenth century to our own, they circulated through the pores of society; they were always hounded, but not always by laws; were often locked up, but not always in prisons; were sick perhaps, but scandalous, dangerous victims, prey to a strange evil that also bore the name of vice and sometimes crime. They were children wise beyond their years, precocious little girls, ambiguous schoolboys, dubious servants and educators, cruel or maniacal husbands, solitary collectors, ramblers with bizarre impulses; they haunted the houses of correction, the penal colonies, the tribunals, and the asylums; they carried their infamy to the doctors and their sickness to the judges. This was the numberless family of perverts who were on friendly terms with delinquents and akin to madmen. In the course of the century they successively bore the stamp of "moral folly," "genital neurosis," "aberration of the genetic instinct," "degenerescence," or "physical imbalance."

What does the appearance of all these peripheral sexualities signify? Is the fact that they could appear in broad daylight a sign that the code had become more lax? Or does the fact that they were given so much attention testify to a stricter regime and to its concern to bring them under close supervision? In terms of repression, things are unclear. There was permissiveness, if one bears in mind that the severity of the codes relating to sexual offenses diminished considerably in the nineteenth century and that law itself often deferred to medicine. But an additional ruse of severity, if one thinks of all the agencies of control and all the mechanisms of surveillance that were put into operation by pedagogy or therapeutics. It may be the case that the intervention of the Church in conjugal sexuality and its rejection of "frauds" against procreation had lost much of their insistence over the previous two hundred years. But medicine made a forceful entry into the pleasures of the couple: it created an entire organic, functional, or mental pathology arising out of "incomplete" sexual practices; it carefully classified all forms of related pleasures; it incorporated them into the notions of "development" and instinctual "disturbances"; and it undertook to manage them.

Perhaps the point to consider is not the level of indulgence or the quantity of repression but the form of power that was exercised. When this whole thicket of disparate sexualities was labeled, as if to disentangle them from one another, was the object to exclude them from reality? It appears, in fact, that the function of the power exerted in this instance was not that of interdiction, and that it involved four operations quite different from simple prohibition.

1. Take the ancient prohibitions of consanguine marriages (as numerous and complex as they were) or the condemnation of adultery, with its inevitable frequency of occurrence; or on the other hand, the recent controls through which, since the nineteenth century, the sexuality of children has been subordinated and their "solitary habits" interfered with. It is clear that we are not dealing with one and the same power mechanism. Not only because in the one case it is a question of law and penality, and in the other, medicine and regimentation; but also because the tactics employed is not the same. On the surface, what appears in both cases is an effort at elimination that was always destined to fail and always constrained to begin again. But the prohibition of "incests" attempted to reach its objective through an asymptotic decrease in the thing it condemned, whereas the control

of infantile sexuality hoped to reach it through a simultaneous propagation of its own power and of the object on
which it was brought to bear. It proceeded in accordance
with a twofold increase extended indefinitely. Educators and
doctors combatted children's onanism like an epidemic that
needed to be eradicated. What this actually entailed,
throughout this whole secular campaign that mobilized the
adult world around the sex of children, was using these
tenuous pleasures as a prop, constituting them as secrets
(that is, forcing them into hiding so as to make possible their
discovery), tracing them back to their source, tracking them
from their origins to their effects, searching out everything
that might cause them or simply enable them to exist. Wherever there was the chance they might appear, devices of
surveillance were installed; traps were laid for compelling
admissions; inexhaustible and corrective discourses were imposed; parents and teachers were alerted, and left with the
suspicion that all children were guilty, and with the fear of
being themselves at fault if their suspicions were not sufficiently strong; they were kept in readiness in the face of this
recurrent danger; their conduct was prescribed and their
pedagogy recodified; an entire medico-sexual regime took
hold of the family milieu. The child's "vice" was not so much
an enemy as a support; it may have been designated as the
evil to be eliminated, but the extraordinary effort that went
into the task that was bound to fail leads one to suspect that
what was demanded of it was to persevere, to proliferate to
the limits of the visible and the invisible, rather than to
disappear for good. Always relying on this support, power
advanced, multiplied its relays and its effects, while its target
expanded, subdivided, and branched out, penetrating further
into reality at the same pace. In appearance, we are dealing
with a barrier system; but in fact, all around the child, indefinite *lines of penetration* were disposed.

2. This new persecution of the peripheral sexualities entailed an *incorporation of perversions* and a new *specification*

of individuals. As defined by the ancient civil or canonical codes, sodomy was a category of forbidden acts; their perpetrator was nothing more than the juridical subject of them. The nineteenth-century homosexual became a personage, a past, a case history, and a childhood, in addition to being a type of life, a life form, and a morphology, with an indiscreet anatomy and possibly a mysterious physiology. Nothing that went into his total composition was unaffected by his sexuality. It was everywhere present in him: at the root of all his actions because it was their insidious and indefinitely active principle; written immodestly on his face and body because it was a secret that always gave itself away. It was consubstantial with him, less as a habitual sin than as a singular nature. We must not forget that the psychological, psychiatric, medical category of homosexuality was constituted from the moment it was characterized—Westphal's famous article of 1870 on "contrary sexual sensations" can stand as its date of birth[1]—less by a type of sexual relations than by a certain quality of sexual sensibility, a certain way of inverting the masculine and the feminine in oneself. Homosexuality appeared as one of the forms of sexuality when it was transposed from the practice of sodomy onto a kind of interior androgyny, a hermaphrodism of the soul. The sodomite had been a temporary aberration; the homosexual was now a species.

So too were all those minor perverts whom nineteenth-century psychiatrists entomologized by giving them strange baptismal names: there were Krafft-Ebing's zoophiles and zooerasts, Rohleder's auto-monosexualists; and later, mixoscopophiles, gynecomasts, presbyophiles, sexoesthetic inverts, and dyspareunist women. These fine names for heresies referred to a nature that was overlooked by the law, but not so neglectful of itself that it did not go on producing more species, even where there was no order to fit them into. The

[1]Carl Westphal, *Archiv für Neurologie,* 1870.

machinery of power that focused on this whole alien strain did not aim to suppress it, but rather to give it an analytical, visible, and permanent reality: it was implanted in bodies, slipped in beneath modes of conduct, made into a principle of classification and intelligibility, established as a *raison d'être* and a natural order of disorder. Not the exclusion of these thousand aberrant sexualities, but the specification, the regional solidification of each one of them. The strategy behind this dissemination was to strew reality with them and incorporate them into the individual.

3. More than the old taboos, this form of power demanded constant, attentive, and curious presences for its exercise; it presupposed proximities; it proceeded through examination and insistent observation; it required an exchange of discourses, through questions that extorted admissions, and confidences that went beyond the questions that were asked. It implied a physical proximity and an interplay of intense sensations. The medicalization of the sexually peculiar was both the effect and the instrument of this. Imbedded in bodies, becoming deeply characteristic of individuals, the oddities of sex relied on a technology of health and pathology. And conversely, since sexuality was a medical and medicalizable object, one had to try and detect it—as a lesion, a dysfunction, or a symptom—in the depths of the organism, or on the surface of the skin, or among all the signs of behavior. The power which thus took charge of sexuality set about contacting bodies, caressing them with its eyes, intensifying areas, electrifying surfaces, dramatizing troubled moments. It wrapped the sexual body in its embrace. There was undoubtedly an increase in effectiveness and an extension of the domain controlled; but also a sensualization of power and a gain of pleasure. This produced a twofold effect: an impetus was given to power through its very exercise; an emotion rewarded the overseeing control and carried it further; the intensity of the confession renewed the questioner's curiosity; the pleasure discovered fed back to the power that encir-

cled it. But so many pressing questions singularized the pleasures felt by the one who had to reply. They were fixed by a gaze, isolated and animated by the attention they received. Power operated as a mechanism of attraction; it drew out those peculiarities over which it kept watch. Pleasure spread to the power that harried it; power anchored the pleasure it uncovered.

The medical examination, the psychiatric investigation, the pedagogical report, and family controls may have the over-all and apparent objective of saying no to all wayward or unproductive sexualities, but the fact is that they function as mechanisms with a double impetus: <u>pleasure</u> and <u>power</u>. The pleasure that comes of exercising a power that questions, monitors, watches, spies, searches out, palpates, brings to light; and on the other hand, the pleasure that kindles at having to evade this power, flee from it, fool it, or travesty it. The power that lets itself be invaded by the pleasure it is pursuing; and opposite it, power asserting itself in the pleasure of showing off, scandalizing, or resisting. Capture and seduction, confrontation and mutual reinforcement: parents and children, adults and adolescents, educator and students, doctors and patients, the psychiatrist with his hysteric and his perverts, all have played this game continually since the nineteenth century. These attractions, these evasions, these circular incitements have traced around bodies and sexes, not boundaries not to be crossed, but *perpetual spirals of power and pleasure*.

4. Whence those *devices of sexual saturation* so characteristic of the space and the social rituals of the nineteenth century. People often say that modern society has attempted to reduce sexuality to the couple—the heterosexual and, insofar as possible, legitimate couple. There are equal grounds for saying that it has, if not created, at least outfitted and made to proliferate, groups with multiple elements and a circulating sexuality: a distribution of points of power, hierarchized and placed opposite to one another; "pursued"

pleasures, that is, both sought after and searched out; compartmental sexualities that are tolerated or encouraged; proximities that serve as surveillance procedures, and function as mechanisms of intensification; contacts that operate as inductors. This is the way things worked in the case of the family, or rather the household, with parents, children, and in some instances, servants. Was the nineteenth-century family really a monogamic and conjugal cell? Perhaps to a certain extent. But it was also a network of pleasures and powers linked together at multiple points and according to transformable relationships. The separation of grown-ups and children, the polarity established between the parents' bedroom and that of the children (it became routine in the course of the century when working-class housing construction was undertaken), the relative segregation of boys and girls, the strict instructions as to the care of nursing infants (maternal breast-feeding, hygiene), the attention focused on infantile sexuality, the supposed dangers of masturbation, the importance attached to puberty, the methods of surveillance suggested to parents, the exhortations, secrets, and fears, the presence—both valued and feared—of servants: all this made the family, even when brought down to its smallest dimensions, a complicated network, saturated with multiple, fragmentary, and mobile sexualities. To reduce them to the conjugal relationship, and then to project the latter, in the form of a forbidden desire, onto the children, cannot account for this apparatus which, in relation to these sexualities, was less a principle of inhibition than an inciting and multiplying mechanism. Educational or psychiatric institutions, with their large populations, their hierarchies, their spatial arrangements, their surveillance systems, constituted, alongside the family, another way of distributing the interplay of powers and pleasures; but they too delineated areas of extreme sexual saturation, with privileged spaces or rituals such as the classroom, the dormitory, the visit, and the consultation. The forms of a nonconjugal, nonmonogamous sexuality were drawn there and established.

Nineteenth-century "bourgeois" society—and it is doubtless still with us—was a society of blatant and fragmented
perversion. And this was not by way of hypocrisy, for nothing was more manifest and more prolix, or more manifestly
taken over by discourses and institutions. Not because, having tried to erect too rigid or too general a barrier against
sexuality, society succeeded only in giving rise to a whole
perverse outbreak and a long pathology of the sexual instinct.
At issue, rather, is the type of power it brought to bear on
the body and on sex. In point of fact, this power had neither
the form of the law, nor the effects of the taboo. On the
contrary, it acted by multiplication of singular sexualities. It
did not set boundaries for sexuality; it extended the various
forms of sexuality, pursuing them according to lines of indefinite penetration. It did not exclude sexuality, but included it
in the body as a mode of specification of individuals. It did
not seek to avoid it; it attracted its varieties by means of
spirals in which pleasure and power reinforced one another.
It did not set up a barrier; it provided places of maximum
saturation. It produced and determined the sexual mosaic.
Modern society is perverse, not in spite of its puritanism or
as if from a backlash provoked by its hypocrisy; it is in actual
fact, and directly, perverse.

In actual fact. The manifold sexualities—those which appear with the different ages (sexualities of the infant or the
child), those which become fixated on particular tastes or
practices (the sexuality of the invert, the gerontophile, the
fetishist), those which, in a diffuse manner, invest relationships (the sexuality of doctor and patient, teacher and student, psychiatrist and mental patient), those which haunt
spaces (the sexuality of the home, the school, the prison)—
all form the correlate of exact procedures of power. We must
not imagine that all these things that were formerly tolerated
attracted notice and received a pejorative designation when
the time came to give a regulative role to the one type of
sexuality that was capable of reproducing labor power and
the form of the family. These polymorphous conducts were

actually extracted from people's bodies and from their pleasures; or rather, they were solidified in them; they were drawn out, revealed, isolated, intensified, incorporated, by multifarious power devices. The growth of perversions is not a moralizing theme that obssessed the scrupulous minds of the Victorians. It is the real product of the encroachment of a type of power on bodies and their pleasures. It is possible that the West has not been capable of inventing any new pleasures, and it has doubtless not discovered any original vices. But it has defined new rules for the game of powers and pleasures. The frozen countenance of the perversions is a fixture of this game.

Directly. This implantation of multiple perversions is not a mockery of sexuality taking revenge on a power that has thrust on it an excessively repressive law. Neither are we dealing with paradoxical forms of pleasure that turn back on power and invest it in the form of a "pleasure to be endured." The implantation of perversions is an instrument-effect: it is through the isolation, intensification, and consolidation of peripheral sexualities that the relations of power to sex and pleasure branched out and multiplied, measured the body, and penetrated modes of conduct. And accompanying this encroachment of powers, scattered sexualities rigidified, became stuck to an age, a place, a type of practice. A proliferation of sexualities through the extension of power; an optimization of the power to which each of these local sexualities gave a surface of intervention: this concatenation, particularly since the nineteenth century, has been ensured and relayed by the countless economic interests which, with the help of medicine, psychiatry, prostitution, and pornography, have tapped into both this analytical multiplication of pleasure and this optimization of the power that controls it. Pleasure and power do not cancel or turn back against one another; they seek out, overlap, and reinforce one another. They are linked together by complex mechanisms and devices of excitation and incitement.

We must therefore abandon the hypothesis that modern industrial societies ushered in an age of increased sexual repression. We have not only witnessed a visible explosion of unorthodox sexualities; but—and this is the important point —a deployment quite different from the law, even if it is locally dependent on procedures of prohibition, has ensured, through a network of interconnecting mechanisms, the proliferation of specific pleasures and the multiplication of disparate sexualities. It is said that no society has been more prudish; never have the agencies of power taken such care to feign ignorance of the thing they prohibited, as if they were determined to have nothing to do with it. But it is the opposite that has become apparent, at least after a general review of the facts: never have there existed more centers of power; never more attention manifested and verbalized; never more circular contacts and linkages; never more sites where the intensity of pleasures and the persistency of power catch hold, only to spread elsewhere.

PART THREE

Scientia Sexualis

I suppose that the first two points will be granted me; I imagine that people will accept my saying that, for two centuries now, the discourse on sex has been multiplied rather than rarefied; and that if it has carried with it taboos and prohibitions, it has also, in a more fundamental way, ensured the solidification and implantation of an entire sexual mosaic. Yet the impression remains that all this has by and large played only a defensive role. By speaking about it so much, by discovering it multiplied, partitioned off, and specified precisely where one had placed it, what one was seeking essentially was simply to conceal sex: a screen-discourse, a dispersion-avoidance. Until Freud at least, the discourse on sex—the discourse of scholars and theoreticians—never ceased to hide the thing it was speaking about. We could take all these things that were said, the painstaking precautions and detailed analyses, as so many procedures meant to evade the unbearable, too hazardous truth of sex. And the mere fact that one claimed to be speaking about it from the rarefied and neutral viewpoint of a science is in itself significant. This was in fact a science made up of evasions since, given its inability or refusal to speak of sex itself, it concerned itself primarily with aberrations, perversions, exceptional oddities, pathological abatements, and morbid aggravations. It was by the same token a science subordinated in the main to the imperatives of a morality whose divisions it reiterated under the guise of the medical norm. Claiming to speak the truth, it stirred up people's fears; to the least oscillations of sexuality, it ascribed an imaginary dynasty of evils destined to be passed on for generations; it declared the furtive customs of the timid, and the most solitary of petty manias, dangerous

53

for the whole society; strange pleasures, it warned, would eventually result in nothing short of death: that of individuals, generations, the species itself.

It thus became associated with an insistent and indiscreet medical practice, glibly proclaiming its aversions, quick to run to the rescue of law and public opinion, more servile with respect to the powers of order than amenable to the requirements of truth. Involuntarily naïve in the best of cases, more often intentionally mendacious, in complicity with what it denounced, haughty and coquettish, it established an entire pornography of the morbid, which was characteristic of the *fin de siècle* society. In France, doctors like Garnier, Pouillet, and Ladoucette were its unglorified scribes and Rollinat its poet. But beyond these troubled pleasures, it assumed other powers; it set itself up as the supreme authority in matters of hygienic necessity, taking up the old fears of venereal affliction and combining them with the new themes of asepsis, and the great evolutionist myths with the recent institutions of public health; it claimed to ensure the physical vigor and the moral cleanliness of the social body; it promised to eliminate defective individuals, degenerate and bastardized populations. In the name of a biological and historical urgency, it justified the racisms of the state, which at the time were on the horizon. It grounded them in "truth."

When we compare these discourses on human sexuality with what was known at the time about the physiology of animal and plant reproduction, we are struck by the incongruity. Their feeble content from the standpoint of elementary rationality, not to mention scientificity, earns them a place apart in the history of knowledge. They form a strangely muddled zone. Throughout the nineteenth century, sex seems to have been incorporated into two very distinct orders of knowledge: a biology of reproduction, which developed continuously according to a general scientific normativity, and a medicine of sex conforming to quite different rules of formation. From one to the other, there was no real exchange, no reciprocal structuration; the role of the first with respect to the second was scarcely more than as a distant and quite fictitious guarantee: a blanket guarantee under cover of which moral obstacles, economic or political options, and traditional fears could be recast in a scientific-sounding vocabulary. It is as if a fundamental resistance blocked the development of a rationally formed discourse concerning human sex, its correlations, and its effects. A disparity of this sort would indicate that the aim of such a discourse was not to state the truth but to prevent its very emergence. Underlying the difference between the physiology of reproduction and the medical theories of sexuality, we would have to see something other and something more than an uneven scientific development or a disparity in the forms of rationality; the one would partake of that immense will to knowledge which has sustained the establishment of scientific discourse in the West, whereas the other would derive from a stubborn will to nonknowledge.

This much is undeniable: the learned discourse on sex that was pronounced in the nineteenth century was imbued with age-old delusions, but also with systematic blindnesses: a refusal to see and to understand; but further—and this is the crucial point—a refusal concerning the very thing that was brought to light and whose formulation was urgently solicited. For there can be no misunderstanding that is not based on a fundamental relation to truth. Evading this truth, barring access to it, masking it: these were so many local tactics which, as if by superimposition and through a last-minute detour, gave a paradoxical form to a fundamental petition to know. Choosing not to recognize was yet another vagary of the will to truth. Let Charcot's Salpêtrière serve as an example in this regard: it was an enormous apparatus for observation, with its examinations, interrogations, and experiments, but it was also a machinery for incitement, with its public presentations, its theater of ritual crises, carefully staged with the help of ether or amyl nitrate, its interplay of dialogues, palpations, laying on of hands, postures which the doctors elicited or obliterated with a gesture or a word, its hierarchy of personnel who kept watch, organized, provoked, monitored, and reported, and who accumulated an immense pyramid of observations and dossiers. It is in the context of this continuous incitement to discourse and to truth that the real mechanisms of misunderstanding *(méconnaissance)* operated: thus Charcot's gesture interrupting a public consultation where it began to be too manifestly a question of "that"; and the more frequent practice of deleting from the succession of dossiers what had been said and demonstrated by the patients regarding sex, but also what had been seen, provoked, solicited by the doctors themselves, things that were almost entirely omitted from the published observations.[1] The important thing, in this affair, is not that these men shut their eyes or stopped their ears, or that they were mistaken; it is rather that they constructed around and apropos of sex an immense apparatus for producing truth, even if this truth was to be masked at the last moment. The essential point is that sex was not only a matter of sensation and pleasure, of law and taboo, but also of truth and falsehood, that the truth of sex became something fundamental, useful, or dangerous, precious or formidable: in short, that sex was constituted as a problem of truth. What needs to be situated, therefore, is not the threshold of a new rationality whose discovery was marked by Freud—or someone else—but the progressive formation (and also the transformations)

[1]Cf., for example, Désiré Bourneville, *Iconographie photographique de la Salpêtrière* (1878–1881), pp. 110 ff. The unpublished documents dealing with the lessons of Charcot, which can still be found at the Salpêtrière, are again more explicit on this point than the published texts. The interplay of incitement and elision is clearly evident in them. A handwritten note gives an account of the session of November 25, 1877. The subject exhibits hysterical spasms; Charcot suspends an attack by placing first his hand, then the end of a baton, on the woman's ovaries. He withdraws the baton, and there is a fresh attack, which he accelerates by administering inhalations of amyl nitrate. The afflicted woman then cries out for the sex-baton in words that are devoid of any metaphor: "G. is taken away and her delirium continues."

of that "interplay of truth and sex" which was bequeathed to us by the nineteenth century, and which we may have modified, but, lacking evidence to the contrary, have not rid ourselves of. Misunderstandings, avoidances, and evasions were only possible, and only had their effects, against the background of this strange endeavor: to tell the truth of sex. An endeavor that does not date from the nineteenth century, even if it was then that a nascent science lent it a singular form. It was the basis of all the aberrant, naïve, and cunning discourses where knowledge of sex seems to have strayed for such a long time.

Historically, there have been two great procedures for producing the truth of sex.

On the one hand, the societies—and they are numerous: China, Japan, India, Rome, the Arabo-Moslem societies—which endowed themselves with an *ars erotica*. In the erotic art, truth is drawn from pleasure itself, understood as a practice and accumulated as experience; pleasure is not considered in relation to an absolute law of the permitted and the forbidden, nor by reference to a criterion of utility, but first and foremost in relation to itself; it is experienced as pleasure, evaluated in terms of its intensity, its specific quality, its duration, its reverberations in the body and the soul. Moreover, this knowledge must be deflected back into the sexual practice itself, in order to shape it as though from within and amplify its effects. In this way, there is formed a knowledge that must remain secret, not because of an element of infamy that might attach to its object, but because of the need to hold it in the greatest reserve, since, according to tradition, it would lose its effectiveness and its virtue by being divulged. Consequently, the relationship to the master who holds the secrets is of paramount importance; only he, working alone, can transmit this art in an esoteric manner and as the culmination of an initiation in which he guides the disciple's progress with unfailing skill and severity. The

effects of this masterful art, which are considerably more
generous than the spareness of its prescriptions would lead
one to imagine, are said to transfigure the one fortunate
enough to receive its privileges: an absolute mastery of the
body, a singular bliss, obliviousness to time and limits, the
elixir of life, the exile of death and its threats.

On the face of it at least, our civilization possesses no *ars
erotica.* In return, it is undoubtedly the only civilization to
practice a *scientia sexualis;* or rather, the only civilization to
have developed over the centuries procedures for telling the
truth of sex which are geared to a form of knowledge-power
strictly opposed to the art of initiations and the masterful
secret: I have in mind the confession.

Since the Middle Ages at least, Western societies have
established the confession as one of the main rituals we rely
on for the production of truth: the codification of the sacrament of penance by the Lateran Council in 1215, with the
resulting development of confessional techniques, the declin-
ing importance of accusatory procedures in criminal justice,
the abandonment of tests of guilt (sworn statements, duels,
judgments of God) and the development of methods of interrogation and inquest, the increased participation of the royal
administration in the prosecution of infractions, at the expense of proceedings leading to private settlements, the setting up of tribunals of Inquisition: all this helped to give the
confession a central role in the order of civil and religious
powers. The evolution of the word *avowal* and of the legal
function it designated is itself emblematic of this development: from being a guarantee of the status, identity, and
value granted to one person by another, it came to signify
someone's acknowledgment of his own actions and thoughts.
For a long time, the individual was vouched for by the reference of others and the demonstration of his ties to the com-
monweal (family, allegiance, protection); then he was
authenticated by the discourse of truth he was able or obliged
to pronounce concerning himself. The truthful confession

was inscribed at the heart of the procedures of individualization by power.

In any case, next to the testing rituals, next to the testimony of witnesses, and the learned methods of observation and demonstration, the confession became one of the West's most highly valued techniques for producing truth. We have since become a singularly confessing society. The confession has spread its effects far and wide. It plays a part in justice, medicine, education, family relationships, and love relations, in the most ordinary affairs of everyday life, and in the most solemn rites; one confesses one's crimes, one's sins, one's thoughts and desires, one's illnesses and troubles; one goes about telling, with the greatest precision, whatever is most difficult to tell. One confesses in public and in private, to one's parents, one's educators, one's doctor, to those one loves; one admits to oneself, in pleasure and in pain, things it would be impossible to tell to anyone else, the things people write books about. One confesses—or is forced to confess. When it is not spontaneous or dictated by some internal imperative, the confession is wrung from a person by violence or threat; it is driven from its hiding place in the soul, or extracted from the body. Since the Middle Ages, torture has accompanied it like a shadow, and supported it when it could go no further: the dark twins.[2] The most defenseless tenderness and the bloodiest of powers have a similar need of confession. Western man has become a confessing animal.

Whence a metamorphosis in literature: we have passed from a pleasure to be recounted and heard, centering on the heroic or marvelous narration of "trials" of bravery or sainthood, to a literature ordered according to the infinite task of extracting from the depths of oneself, in between the words, a truth which the very form of the confession holds out like a shimmering mirage. Whence too this new way of philosophizing: seeking the fundamental relation to the true, not

[2] Greek law had already coupled torture and confession, at least where slaves were concerned, and Imperial Roman law had widened the practice.

simply in oneself—in some forgotten knowledge, or in a certain primal trace—but in the self-examination that yields, through a multitude of fleeting impressions, the basic certainties of consciousness. The obligation to confess is now relayed through so many different points, is so deeply ingrained in us, that we no longer perceive it as the effect of a power that constrains us; on the contrary, it seems to us that truth, lodged in our most secret nature, "demands" only to surface; that if it fails to do so, this is because a constraint holds it in place, the violence of a power weighs it down, and it can finally be articulated only at the price of a kind of liberation. Confession frees, but power reduces one to silence; truth does not belong to the order of power, but shares an original affinity with freedom: traditional themes in philosophy, which a "political history of truth" would have to overturn by showing that truth is not by nature free—nor error servile—but that its production is thoroughly imbued with relations of power. The confession is an example of this.

One has to be completely taken in by this internal ruse of confession in order to attribute a fundamental role to censorship, to taboos regarding speaking and thinking; one has to have an inverted image of power in order to believe that all these voices which have spoken so long in our civilization—repeating the formidable injunction to tell what one is and what one does, what one recollects and what one has forgotten, what one is thinking and what one thinks he is not thinking—are speaking to us of freedom. An immense labor to which the West has submitted generations in order to produce—while other forms of work ensured the accumulation of capital—men's subjection: their constitution as subjects in both senses of the word. Imagine how exorbitant must have seemed the order given to all Christians at the beginning of the thirteenth century, to kneel at least once a year and confess to all their transgressions, without omitting a single one. And think of that obscure partisan, seven centuries later, who had come to rejoin the Serbian resistance deep

in the mountains; his superiors asked him to write his life
story; and when he brought them a few miserable pages,
scribbled in the night, they did not look at them but only said
to him, "Start over, and tell the truth." Should those much-
discussed language taboos make us forget this millennial
yoke of confession?

From the Christian penance to the present day, sex was a
privileged theme of confession. A thing that was hidden, we
are told. But what if, on the contrary, it was what, in a quite
particular way, one confessed? Suppose the obligation to
conceal it was but another aspect of the duty to admit to it
(concealing it all the more and with greater care as the
confession of it was more important, requiring a stricter
ritual and promising more decisive effects)? What if sex in
our society, on a scale of several centuries, was something
that was placed within an unrelenting system of confession?
The transformation of sex into discourse, which I spoke of
earlier, the dissemination and reinforcement of heterogeneous sexualities, are perhaps two elements of the same deployment: they are linked together with the help of the central
element of a confession that compels individuals to articulate
their sexual peculiarity—no matter how extreme. In Greece,
truth and sex were linked, in the form of pedagogy, by the
transmission of a precious knowledge from one body to another; sex served as a medium for initiations into learning.
For us, it is in the confession that truth and sex are joined,
through the obligatory and exhaustive expression of an individual secret. But this time it is truth that serves as a medium
for sex and its manifestations.

The confession is a ritual of discourse in which the speaking subject is also the subject of the statement; it is also a
ritual that unfolds within a power relationship, for one does
not confess without the presence (or virtual presence) of a
partner who is not simply the interlocutor but the authority
who requires the confession, prescribes and appreciates it,
and intervenes in order to judge, punish, forgive, console,

and reconcile; a ritual in which the truth is corroborated by the obstacles and resistances it has had to surmount in order to be formulated; and finally, a ritual in which the expression alone, independently of its external consequences, produces intrinsic modifications in the person who articulates it: it exonerates, redeems, and purifies him; it unburdens him of his wrongs, liberates him, and promises him salvation. For centuries, the truth of sex was, at least for the most part, caught up in this discursive form. Moreover, this form was not the same as that of education (sexual education confined itself to general principles and rules of prudence); nor was it that of initiation (which remained essentially a silent practice, which the act of sexual enlightenment or deflowering merely rendered laughable or violent). As we have seen, it is a form that is far removed from the one governing the "erotic art." By virtue of the power structure immanent in it, the confessional discourse cannot come from above, as in the *ars erotica,* through the sovereign will of a master, but rather from below, as an obligatory act of speech which, under some imperious compulsion, breaks the bonds of discretion or forgetfulness. What secrecy it presupposes is not owing to the high price of what it has to say and the small number of those who are worthy of its benefits, but to its obscure familiarity and its general baseness. Its veracity is not guaranteed by the lofty authority of the magistery, nor by the tradition it transmits, but by the bond, the basic intimacy in discourse, between the one who speaks and what he is speaking about. On the other hand, the agency of domination does not reside in the one who speaks (for it is he who is constrained), but in the one who listens and says nothing; not in the one who knows and answers, but in the one who questions and is not supposed to know. And this discourse of truth finally takes effect, not in the one who receives it, but in the one from whom it is wrested. With these confessed truths, we are a long way from the learned initiations into pleasure, with their technique and their mystery. On the other hand, we belong to a society which has ordered sex's difficult knowledge, not according to the transmission of secrets, but around the slow surfacing of confidential statements.

The confession was, and still remains, the general standard governing the production of the true discourse on sex. It has undergone a considerable transformation, however. For a long time, it remained firmly entrenched in the practice of penance. But with the rise of Protestantism, the Counter Reformation, eighteenth-century pedagogy, and nineteenth-century medicine, it gradually lost its ritualistic and exclusive localization; it spread; it has been employed in a whole series of relationships: children and parents, students and educators, patients and psychiatrists, delinquents and experts. The motivations and effects it is expected to produce have varied, as have the forms it has taken: interrogations, consultations, autobiographical narratives, letters; they have been recorded, transcribed, assembled into dossiers, published, and commented on. But more important, the confession lends itself, if not to other domains, at least to new ways of exploring the existing ones. It is no longer a question simply of saying what was done—the sexual act—and how it was done; but of reconstructing, in and around the act, the thoughts that recapitulated it, the obsessions that accompanied it, the images, desires, modulations, and quality of the pleasure that animated it. For the first time no doubt, a society has taken upon itself to solicit and hear the imparting of individual pleasures.

A dissemination, then, of procedures of confession, a multiple localization of their constraint, a widening of their domain: a great archive of the pleasures of sex was gradually constituted. For a long time this archive dematerialized as it was formed. It regularly disappeared without a trace (thus suiting the purposes of the Christian pastoral) until medicine, psychiatry, and pedagogy began to solidify it: Campe, Salzmann, and especially Kaan, Krafft-Ebing, Tardieu, Molle, and Havelock Ellis carefully assembled this whole pitiful, lyrical outpouring from the sexual mosaic. Western societies thus began to keep an indefinite record of these people's pleasures. They made up a herbal of them and established a system of classification. They described their everyday deficiencies as well as their oddities or exasperations. This was an important time. It is easy to make light of these nineteenth-century psychiatrists, who made a point of apologizing for the horrors they were about to let speak, evoking "immoral behavior" or "aberrations of the genetic senses," but I am more inclined to applaud their seriousness: they had a feeling for momentous events. It was a time when the most singular pleasures were called upon to pronounce a discourse of truth concerning themselves, a discourse which had to model itself after that which spoke, not of sin and salvation, but of bodies and life processes—the discourse of science. It was enough to make one's voice tremble, for an improbable thing was then taking shape: a confessional science, a science which relied on a many-sided extortion, and took for its object what was unmentionable but admitted to nonetheless. The scientific discourse was scandalized, or in any case repelled, when it had to take charge of this whole discourse from below. It was also faced with a theoretical and methodological paradox: the long discussions concerning the possibility of constituting a science of the subject, the validity of introspection, lived experience as evidence, or the presence of consciousness to itself were responses to this problem that is inherent in the functioning of truth in our society: can one articulate the production of truth according to the old juridico-religious model of confession, and the extortion of confidential evidence according to the rules of scientific discourse? Those who believe that sex was more rigorously elided in the nineteenth century than ever before, through a formidable mechanism of blockage and a deficiency of discourse, can say what they please. There was no deficiency, but rather an excess, a redoubling, too much rather than not enough discourse, in any case an interference between two modes of production of truth: procedures of confession, and scientific discursivity.

And instead of adding up the errors, naïvetés, and moralisms that plagued the nineteenth-century discourse of truth concerning sex, we would do better to locate the procedures by which that will to knowledge regarding sex, which characterizes the modern Occident, caused the rituals of confession to function within the norms of scientific regularity: how did this immense and traditional extortion of the sexual confession come to be constituted in scientific terms?

1. *Through a clinical codification of the inducement to speak.* Combining confession with examination, the personal history with the deployment of a set of decipherable signs and symptoms; the interrogation, the exacting questionnaire, and hypnosis, with the recollection of memories and free association: all were ways of reinscribing the procedure of confession in a field of scientifically acceptable observations.

2. *Through the postulate of a general and diffuse causality.* Having to tell everything, being able to pose questions about everything, found their justification in the principle that endowed sex with an inexhaustible and polymorphous causal power. The most discrete event in one's sexual behavior— whether an accident or a deviation, a deficit or an excess— was deemed capable of entailing the most varied consequences throughout one's existence; there was scarcely a malady or physical disturbance to which the nineteenth century did not impute at least some degree of sexual etiology. From the bad habits of children to the phthises of adults, the apoplexies of old people, nervous maladies, and the degenerations of the race, the medicine of that era wove an entire network of sexual causality to explain them. This may well appear fantastic to us, but the principle of sex as a "cause of any and everything" was the theoretical underside of a confession that had to be thorough, meticulous, and constant,

and at the same time operate within a scientific type of practice. The limitless dangers that sex carried with it justified the exhaustive character of the inquisition to which it was subjected.

3. *Through the principle of a latency intrinsic to sexuality.* If it was necessary to extract the truth of sex through the technique of confession, this was not simply because it was difficult to tell, or stricken by the taboos of decency, but because the ways of sex were obscure; it was elusive by nature; its energy and its mechanisms escaped observation, and its causal power was partly clandestine. By integrating it into the beginnings of a scientific discourse, the nineteenth century altered the scope of the confession; it tended no longer to be concerned solely with what the subject wished to hide, but with what was hidden from himself, being incapable of coming to light except gradually and through the labor of a confession in which the questioner and the questioned each had a part to play. The principle of a latency essential to sexuality made it possible to link the forcing of a difficult confession to a scientific practice. It had to be exacted, by force, since it involved something that tried to stay hidden.

4. *Through the method of interpretation.* If one had to confess, this was not merely because the person to whom one confessed had the power to forgive, console, and direct, but because the work of producing the truth was obliged to pass through this relationship if it was to be scientifically validated. The truth did not reside solely in the subject who, by confessing, would reveal it wholly formed. It was constituted in two stages: present but incomplete, blind to itself, in the one who spoke, it could only reach completion in the one who assimilated and recorded it. It was the latter's function to verify this obscure truth: the revelation of confession had to be coupled with the decipherment of what it said. The one

who listened was not simply the forgiving master, the judge who condemned or acquitted; he was the master of truth. His was a hermaneutic function. With regard to the confession, his power was not only to demand it before it was made, or decide what was to follow after it, but also to constitute a discourse of truth on the basis of its decipherment. By no longer making the confession a test, but rather a sign, and by making sexuality something to be interpreted, the nineteenth century gave itself the possibility of causing the procedures of confession to operate within the regular formation of a scientific discourse.

5. *Through the medicalization of the effects of confession.* The obtaining of the confession and its effects were recodified as therapeutic operations. Which meant first of all that the sexual domain was no longer accounted for simply by the notions of error or sin, excess or transgression, but was placed under the rule of the normal and the pathological (which, for that matter, were the transposition of the former categories); a characteristic sexual morbidity was defined for the first time; sex appeared as an extremely unstable pathological field: a surface of repercussion for other ailments, but also the focus of a specific nosography, that of instincts, tendencies, images, pleasure, and conduct. This implied furthermore that sex would derive its meaning and its necessity from medical interventions: it would be required by the doctor, necessary for diagnosis, and effective by nature in the cure. Spoken in time, to the proper party, and by the person who was both the bearer of it and the one responsible for it, the truth healed.

Let us consider things in broad historical perspective: breaking with the traditions of the *ars erotica,* our society has equipped itself with a *scientia sexualis.* To be more precise, it has pursued the task of producing true discourses concerning sex, and this by adapting—not without difficulty—the

ancient procedure of confession to the rules of scientific discourse. Paradoxically, the *scientia sexualis* that emerged in
the nineteenth century kept as its nucleus the singular ritual
of obligatory and exhaustive confession, which in the Christian West was the first technique for producing the truth of
sex. Beginning in the sixteenth century, this rite gradually
detached itself from the sacrament of penance, and via the
guidance of souls and the direction of conscience—the *ars
artium*—emigrated toward pedagogy, relationships between
adults and children, family relations, medicine, and psychiatry. In any case, nearly one hundred and fifty years have gone
into the making of a complex machinery for producing true
discourses on sex: a deployment that spans a wide segment
of history in that it connects the ancient injunction of confession to clinical listening methods. It is this deployment that
enables something called "sexuality" to embody the truth of
sex and its pleasures.

"Sexuality": the correlative of that slowly developed discursive practice which constitutes the *scientia sexualis*. The
essential features of this sexuality are not the expression of
a representation that is more or less distorted by ideology, or
of a misunderstanding caused by taboos; they correspond to
the functional requirements of a discourse that must produce
its truth. Situated at the point of intersection of a technique
of confession and a scientific discursivity, where certain
major mechanisms had to be found for adapting them to one
another (the listening technique, the postulate of causality,
the principle of latency, the rule of interpretation, the imperative of medicalization), sexuality was defined as being "by
nature": a domain susceptible to pathological processes, and
hence one calling for therapeutic or normalizing interventions; a field of meanings to decipher; the site of processes
concealed by specific mechanisms; a focus of indefinite causal
relations; and an obscure speech *(parole)* that had to be
ferreted out and listened to. The "economy" of discourses—
their intrinsic technology, the necessities of their operation,

the tactics they employ, the effects of power which underlie them and which they transmit—this, and not a system of representations, is what determines the essential features of what they have to say. The history of sexuality—that is, the history of what functioned in the nineteenth century as a specific field of truth—must first be written from the viewpoint of a history of discourses.

Let us put forward a general working hypothesis. The society that emerged in the nineteenth century—bourgeois, capitalist, or industrial society, call it what you will—did not confront sex with a fundamental refusal of recognition. On the contrary, it put into operation an entire machinery for producing true discourses concerning it. Not only did it speak of sex and compel everyone to do so; it also set out to formulate the uniform truth of sex. As if it suspected sex of harboring a fundamental secret. As if it needed this production of truth. As if it was essential that sex be inscribed not only in an economy of pleasure but in an ordered system of knowledge. Thus sex gradually became an object of great suspicion; the general and disquieting meaning that pervades our conduct and our existence, in spite of ourselves; the point of weakness where evil portents reach through to us; the fragment of darkness that we each carry within us: a general signification, a universal secret, an omnipresent cause, a fear that never ends. And so, in this "question" of sex (in both senses: as interrogation and problematization, and as the need for confession and integration into a field of rationality), two processes emerge, the one always conditioning the other: we demand that sex speak the truth (but, since it is the secret and is oblivious to its own nature, we reserve for ourselves the function of telling the truth of its truth, revealed and deciphered at last), and we demand that it tell us our truth, or rather, the deeply buried truth of that truth about ourselves which we think we possess in our immediate consciousness. We tell it its truth by deciphering what it tells us about that truth; it tells us our own by delivering up that part of it that escaped us. From this interplay there has evolved, over several centuries, a knowledge of the subject; a knowledge not so much of his form, but of that which divides him, determines him perhaps, but above all causes him to be ignorant of himself. As unlikely as this may seem, it should not surprise us when we think of the long history of the Christian and juridical confession, of the shifts and transformations this form of knowledge-power, so important in the West, has undergone: the project of a science of the subject has gravitated, in ever narrowing circles, around the question of sex. Causality in the subject, the unconscious of the subject, the truth of the subject in the other who knows, the knowledge he holds unbeknown to him, all this found an opportunity to deploy itself in the discourse of sex. Not, however, by reason of some natural property inherent in sex itself, but by virtue of the tactics of power immanent in this discourse.

Scientia sexualis versus *ars erotica,* no doubt. But it should be noted that the *ars erotica* did not disappear altogether from Western civilization; nor has it always been absent from the movement by which one sought to produce a science of sexuality. In the Christian confession, but especially in the direction and examination of conscience, in the search for spiritual union and the love of God, there was a whole series of methods that had much in common with an erotic art: guidance by the master along a path of initiation, the intensification of experiences extending down to their physical components, the optimization of effects by the discourse that accompanied them. The phenomena of possession and ecstasy, which were quite frequent in the Catholicism of the Counter Reformation, were undoubtedly effects that had got outside the control of the erotic technique immanent in this subtle science of the flesh. And we must ask whether, since the nineteenth century, the *scientia sexualis*—under the guise of its decent positivism—has not functioned, at least to

Scientia Sexualis 71

a certain extent, as an *ars erotica.* Perhaps this production
of truth, intimidated though it was by the scientific model,
multiplied, intensified, and even created its own intrinsic
pleasures. It is often said that we have been incapable of
imagining any new pleasures. We have at least invented a
different kind of pleasure: pleasure in the truth of pleasure,
the pleasure of knowing that truth, of discovering and exposing it, the fascination of seeing it and telling it, of captivating
and capturing others by it, of confiding it in secret, of luring
it out in the open—the specific pleasure of the true discourse
on pleasure.

The most important elements of an erotic art linked to our
knowledge about sexuality are not to be sought in the ideal,
promised to us by medicine, of a healthy sexuality, nor in the
humanist dream of a complete and flourishing sexuality, and
certainly not in the lyricism of orgasm and the good feelings
of bio-energy (these are but aspects of its normalizing utilization), but in this multiplication and intensification of pleasures connected to the production of the truth about sex. The
learned volumes, written and read; the consultations and
examinations; the anguish of answering questions and the
delights of having one's words interpreted; all the stories told
to oneself and to others, so much curiosity, so many confidences offered in the face of scandal, sustained—but not
without trembling a little—by the obligation of truth; the
profusion of secret fantasies and the dearly paid right to
whisper them to whoever is able to hear them; in short, the
formidable "pleasure of analysis" (in the widest sense of the
latter term) which the West has cleverly been fostering for
several centuries: all this constitutes something like the er-
rant fragments of an erotic art that is secretly transmitted by
confession and the science of sex. Must we conclude that our
scientia sexualis is but an extraordinarily subtle form of *ars
erotica,* and that it is the Western, sublimated version of that
seemingly lost tradition? Or must we suppose that all these
pleasures are only the by-products of a sexual science, a

bonus that compensates for its many stresses and strains?

In any case, the hypothesis of a power of repression exerted by our society on sex for economic reasons appears to me quite inadequate if we are to explain this whole series of reinforcements and intensifications that our preliminary inquiry has discovered: a proliferation of discourses, carefully tailored to the requirements of power; the solidification of the sexual mosaic and the construction of devices capable not only of isolating it but of stimulating and provoking it, of forming it into focuses of attention, discourse, and pleasure; the mandatory production of confessions and the subsequent establishment of a system of legitimate knowledge and of an economy of manifold pleasures. We are dealing not nearly so much with a negative mechanism of exclusion as with the operation of a subtle network of discourses, special knowledges, pleasures, and powers. At issue is not a movement bent on pushing rude sex back into some obscure and inaccessible region, but on the contrary, a process that spreads it over the surface of things and bodies, arouses it, draws it out and bids it speak, implants it in reality and enjoins it to tell the truth: an entire glittering sexual array, reflected in a myriad of discourses, the obstination of powers, and the interplay of knowledge and pleasure.

All this is an illusion, it will be said, a hasty impression behind which a more discerning gaze will surely discover the same great machinery of repression. Beyond these few phosphorescences, are we not sure to find once more the somber law that always says no? The answer will have to come out of a historical inquiry. An inquiry concerning the manner in which a knowledge of sex has been forming over the last three centuries; the manner in which the discourses that take it as their object have multiplied, and the reasons for which we have come to attach a nearly fabulous price to the truth they claimed to produce. Perhaps these historical analyses will end by dissipating what this cursory survey seems to suggest. But the postulate I started out with, and would like to hold to as long as possible, is that these deployments of power and knowledge, of truth and pleasures, so unlike those of repression, are not necessarily secondary and derivative; and further, that repression is not in any case fundamental and overriding. We need to take these mechanisms seriously, therefore, and reverse the direction of our analysis: rather than assuming a generally acknowledged repression, and an ignorance measured against what we are supposed to know, we must begin with these positive mechanisms, insofar as they produce knowledge, multiply discourse, induce pleasure, and generate power; we must investigate the conditions of their emergence and operation, and try to discover how the related facts of interdiction or concealment are distributed with respect to them. In short, we must define the strategies of power that are immanent in this will to knowledge. As far as sexuality is concerned, we shall attempt to constitute the "political economy" of a will to knowledge.

PART FOUR

The Deployment
of Sexuality

The aim of this series of studies? To transcribe into history the fable of *Les Bijoux indiscrets*.

Among its many emblems, our society wears that of the talking sex. The sex which one catches unawares and questions, and which, restrained and loquacious at the same time, endlessly replies. One day a certain mechanism, which was so elfin-like that it could make itself invisible, captured this sex and, in a game that combined pleasure with compulsion, and consent with inquisition, made it tell the truth about itself and others as well. For many years, we have all been living in the realm of Prince Mangogul: under the spell of an immense curiosity about sex, bent on questioning it, with an insatiable desire to hear it speak and be spoken about, quick to invent all sorts of magical rings that might force it to abandon its discretion. As if it were essential for us to be able to draw from that little piece of ourselves not only pleasure but knowledge, and a whole subtle interchange from one to the other: a knowledge of pleasure, a pleasure that comes of knowing pleasure, a knowledge-pleasure; and as if that fantastic animal we accommodate had itself such finely tuned ears, such searching eyes, so gifted a tongue and mind, as to know much and be quite willing to tell it, provided we employed a little skill in urging it to speak. Between each of us and our sex, the West has placed a never-ending demand for truth: it is up to us to extract the truth of sex, since this truth is beyond its grasp; it is up to sex to tell us our truth, since sex is what holds it in darkness. But is sex hidden from us, concealed by a new sense of decency, kept under a bushel by the grim necessities of bourgeois society? On the contrary, it shines forth; it is incandescent. Several centuries ago, it was

placed at the center of a formidable *petition to know.* A
double petition, in that we are compelled to know how things
are with it, while it is suspected of knowing how things are
with us.

In the space of a few centuries, a certain inclination has
led us to direct the question of what we are, to sex. Not so
much to sex as representing nature, but to sex as history, as
signification and discourse. We have placed ourselves under
the sign of sex, but in the form of a *Logic of Sex,* rather than
a *Physics.* We must make no mistake here: with the great
series of binary oppositions (body/soul, flesh/spirit, instinct/
reason, drives/consciousness) that seemed to refer sex to a
pure mechanics devoid of reason, the West has managed not
only, or not so much, to annex sex to a field of rationality,
which would not be all that remarkable an achievement,
seeing how accustomed we are to such "conquests" since the
Greeks, but to bring us almost entirely—our bodies, our
minds, our individuality, our history—under the sway of a
logic of concupiscence and desire. Whenever it is a question
of knowing who we are, it is this logic that henceforth serves
as our master key. It has been several decades since geneti-
cists ceased to conceive of life as an organization strangely
equipped with an additional capacity to reproduce itself; they
see in the reproductive mechanism that very element which
introduces the biological dimension: the matrix not only of
the living, but of life itself. But it was centuries ago that
countless theoreticians and practitioners of the flesh—whose
approach was hardly "scientific," it is true—made man the
offspring of an imperious and intelligible sex. Sex, the explanation for everything.

It is pointless to ask: Why then is sex so secret? What is
this force that so long reduced it to silence and has only
recently relaxed its hold somewhat, allowing us to question
it perhaps, but always in the context of and through its
repression? In reality, this question, so often repeated nowadays, is but the recent form of a considerable affirmation and

a secular prescription: there is where the truth is; go see if you can uncover it. *Acheronto movebo:* an age-old decision.

> *Ye wise men, highly, deeply learned,*
> *Who think it out and know,*
> *How, when, and where do all things pair?*
> *Why do they kiss and love?*
> *Ye men of lofty wisdom, say*
> *What happened to me then;*
> *Search out and tell me where, how, when*
> *And why it happened thus.*[1]

It is reasonable therefore to ask first of all: What is this injunction? Why this great chase after the truth of sex, the truth in sex?

In Diderot's tale, the good genie Cucufa discovers at the bottom of his pocket, in the midst of worthless things—consecrated seeds, little pagodas made of lead, and moldy sugar-coated pills—the tiny silver ring whose stone, when turned, makes the sexes one encounters speak. He gives it to the curious sultan. Our problem is to know what marvelous ring confers a similar power on us, and on which master's finger it has been placed; what game of power it makes possible or presupposes, and how it is that each one of us has become a sort of attentive and imprudent sultan with respect to his own sex and that of others. It is this magical ring, this jewel which is so indiscreet when it comes to making others speak, but so ineloquent concerning one's own mechanism, that we need to render loquacious in its turn; it is what we have to talk about. We must write the history of this will to truth, this petition to know that for so many centuries has kept us enthralled by sex: the history of a stubborn and relentless effort. What is it that we demand of sex, beyond its possible pleasures, that makes us so persistent? What is this patience or eagerness to constitute it as the secret, the

[1]Gottfried August Bürger, cited by Arthur Schopenhauer in *The Metaphysics of the Love of the Sexes.* From *The Will to Live: Selected Writings of Arthur Schopenhauer* (New York: Frederick Ungar, 1962), p.69.

omnipotent cause, the hidden meaning, the unremitting fear? And why was the task of discovering this difficult truth finally turned into an invitation to eliminate taboos and break free of what binds us? Was the labor then so arduous that it had to be enchanted by this promise? Or had this knowledge become so costly—in political, economic, and ethical terms—that in order to subject everyone to its rule, it was necessary to assure them, paradoxically, that their liberation was at stake?

In order to situate the investigations that will follow, let me put forward some general propositions concerning the objective, the method, the domain to be covered, and the periodizations that one can accept in a provisory way.

I

Objective

Why these investigations? I am well aware that an uncertainty runs through the sketches I have drawn thus far, one that threatens to invalidate the more detailed inquiries that I have projected. I have repeatedly stressed that the history of the last centuries in Western societies did not manifest the movement of a power that was essentially repressive. I based my argument on the disqualification of that notion while feigning ignorance of the fact that a critique has been mounted from another quarter and doubtless in a more radical fashion: a critique conducted at the level of the theory of desire. In point of fact, the assertion that sex is not "repressed" is not altogether new. Psychoanalysts have been saying the same thing for some time. They have challenged the simple little machinery that comes to mind when one speaks of repression; the idea of a rebellious energy that must be throttled has appeared to them inadequate for deciphering the manner in which power and desire are joined to one another; they consider them to be linked in a more complex and primary way than through the interplay of a primitive, natural, and living energy welling up from below, and a higher order seeking to stand in its way; thus one should not think that desire is repressed, for the simple reason that the law is what constitutes both desire and the lack on which it is predicated. Where there is desire, the power relation is already present: an illusion, then, to denounce this relation

81

for a repression exerted after the event; but vanity as well, to go questing after a desire that is beyond the reach of power.

But, in an obstinately confused way, I sometimes spoke, as though I were dealing with equivalent notions, of *repression,* and sometimes of *law,* of prohibition or censorship. Through stubbornness or neglect, I failed to consider everything that can distinguish their theoretical implications. And I grant that one might justifiably say to me: By constantly referring to positive technologies of power, you are playing a double game where you hope to win on all counts; you confuse your adversaries by appearing to take the weaker position, and, discussing repression alone, you would have us believe, wrongly, that you have rid yourself of the problem of law; and yet you keep the essential practical consequence of the principle of power-as-law, namely the fact that there is no escaping from power, that it is always-already present, constituting that very thing which one attempts to counter it with. As to the idea of a power-repression, you have retained its most fragile theoretical element, and this in order to criticize it; you have retained the most sterilizing political consequence of the idea of power-law, but only in order to preserve it for your own use.

The aim of the inquiries that will follow is to move less toward a "theory" of power than toward an "analytics" of power: that is, toward a definition of the specific domain formed by relations of power, and toward a determination of the instruments that will make possible its analysis. However, it seems to me that this analytics can be constituted only if it frees itself completely from a certain representation of power that I would term—it will be seen later why—"juridico-discursive." It is this conception that governs both the thematics of repression and the theory of the law as constitutive of desire. In other words, what distinguishes the analysis made in terms of the repression of instincts from that made in terms of the law of desire is clearly the way in which they each conceive of the nature and dynamics of the drives, not the way in which they conceive of power. They both rely on a common representation of power which, depending on the use made of it and the position it is accorded with respect to desire, leads to two contrary results: either to the promise of a "liberation," if power is seen as having only an external hold on desire, or, if it is constitutive of desire itself, to the affirmation: you are always-already trapped. Moreover, one must not imagine that this representation is peculiar to those who are concerned with the problem of the relations of power with sex. In fact it is much more general; one frequently encounters it in political analyses of power, and it is deeply rooted in the history of the West.

These are some of its principal features:

—*The negative relation.* It never establishes any connection between power and sex that is not negative: rejection, exclusion, refusal, blockage, concealment, or mask. Where sex and pleasure are concerned, power can "do" nothing but say no to them; what it produces, if anything, is absences and gaps; it overlooks elements, introduces discontinuities, separates what is joined, and marks off boundaries. Its effects take the general form of limit and lack.

—*The insistence of the rule.* Power is essentially what dictates its law to sex. Which means first of all that sex is placed by power in a binary system: licit and illicit, permitted and forbidden. Secondly, power prescribes an "order" for sex that operates at the same time as a form of intelligibility: sex is to be deciphered on the basis of its relation to the law. And finally, power acts by laying down the rule: power's hold on sex is maintained through language, or rather through the act of discourse that creates, from the very fact that it is articulated, a rule of law. It speaks, and that is the rule. The pure form of power resides in the function of the legislator; and its mode of action with regard to sex is of a juridico-discursive character.

—*The cycle of prohibition:* thou shalt not go near, thou shalt not touch, thou shalt not consume, thou shalt not experience pleasure, thou shalt not speak, thou shalt not show thyself; ultimately thou shalt not exist, except in darkness and secrecy. To deal with sex, power employs nothing more than a law of prohibition. Its objective: that sex renounce itself. Its instrument: the threat of a punishment that is nothing other than the suppression of sex. Renounce yourself or suffer the penalty of being suppressed; do not appear if you do not want to disappear. Your existence will be maintained only at the cost of your nullification. Power constrains sex only through a taboo that plays on the alternative between two nonexistences.

—*The logic of censorship.* This interdiction is thought to take three forms: affirming that such a thing is not permitted, preventing it from being said, denying that it exists. Forms that are difficult to reconcile. But it is here that one imagines a sort of logical sequence that characterizes censorship mechanisms: it links the inexistent, the illicit, and the inexpressible in such a way that each is at the same time the principle and the effect of the others: one must not talk about what is forbidden until it is annulled in reality; what is inexistent has no right to show itself, even in the order of speech where its inexistence is declared; and that which one must keep silent about is banished from reality as the thing that is tabooed above all else. The logic of power exerted on sex is the paradoxical logic of a law that might be expressed as an injunction of nonexistence, nonmanifestation, and silence.

—*The uniformity of the apparatus.* Power over sex is exercised in the same way at all levels. From top to bottom, in its over-all decisions and its capillary interventions alike, whatever the devices or institutions on which it relies, it acts in a uniform and comprehensive manner; it operates according to the simple and endlessly reproduced mechanisms of law, taboo, and censorship: from state to family, from prince to father, from the tribunal to the small change of everyday punishments, from the agencies of social domination to the structures that constitute the subject himself, one finds a general form of power, varying in scale alone. This form is the law of transgression and punishment, with its interplay of licit and illicit. Whether one attributes to it the form of the prince who formulates rights, of the father who forbids, of the censor who enforces silence, or of the master who states the law, in any case one schematizes power in a juridical form, and one defines its effects as obedience. Confronted by a power that is law, the subject who is constituted as subject —who is "subjected"—is he who obeys. To the formal homogeneity of power in these various instances corresponds the general form of submission in the one who is constrained by it—whether the individual in question is the subject opposite the monarch, the citizen opposite the state, the child opposite the parent, or the disciple opposite the master. A legislative power on one side, and an obedient subject on the other.

Underlying both the general theme that power represses sex and the idea that the law constitutes desire, one encounters the same putative mechanics of power. It is defined in a strangely restrictive way, in that, to begin with, this power is poor in resources, sparing of its methods, monotonous in the tactics it utilizes, incapable of invention, and seemingly doomed always to repeat itself. Further, it is a power that only has the force of the negative on its side, a power to say no; in no condition to produce, capable only of posting limits, it is basically anti-energy. This is the paradox of its effectiveness: it is incapable of doing anything, except to render what it dominates incapable of doing anything either, except for what this power allows it to do. And finally, it is a power whose model is essentially juridical, centered on nothing more than the statement of the law and the operation of taboos. All the modes of domination, submission, and subjugation are ultimately reduced to an effect of obedience.

Why is this juridical notion of power, involving as it does the neglect of everything that makes for its productive effectiveness, its strategic resourcefulness, its positivity, so readily accepted? In a society such as ours, where the devices of power are so numerous, its rituals so visible, and its instruments ultimately so reliable, in this society that has been more imaginative, probably, than any other in creating devious and supple mechanisms of power, what explains this tendency not to recognize the latter except in the negative and emaciated form of prohibition? Why are the deployments of power reduced simply to the procedure of the law of interdiction?

Let me offer a general and tactical reason that seems self-evident: power is tolerable only on condition that it mask a substantial part of itself. Its success is proportional to its ability to hide its own mechanisms. Would power be accepted if it were entirely cynical? For it, secrecy is not in the nature of an abuse; it is indispensable to its operation. Not only because power imposes secrecy on those whom it dominates, but because it is perhaps just as indispensable to the latter: would they accept it if they did not see it as a mere limit placed on their desire, leaving a measure of freedom—however slight—intact? Power as a pure limit set on freedom is, at least in our society, the general form of its acceptability.

There is, perhaps, a historical reason for this. The great institutions of power that developed in the Middle Ages—monarchy, the state with its apparatus—rose up on the basis of a multiplicity of prior powers, and to a certain extent in opposition to them: dense, entangled, conflicting powers, powers tied to the direct or indirect dominion over the land, to the possession of arms, to serfdom, to bonds of suzerainty and vassalage. If these institutions were able to implant themselves, if, by profiting from a whole series of tactical alliances, they were able to gain acceptance, this was because they presented themselves as agencies of regulation, arbitration, and demarcation, as a way of introducing order in the midst of these powers, of establishing a principle that would temper them and distribute them according to boundaries and a fixed hierarchy. Faced with a myriad of clashing forces, these great forms of power functioned as a principle of right that transcended all the heterogeneous claims, manifesting the triple distinction of forming a unitary regime, of identifying its will with the law, and of acting through mechanisms of interdiction and sanction. The slogan of this regime, *pax et justitia,* in keeping with the function it laid claim to, established peace as the prohibition of feudal or private wars, and justice as a way of suspending the private settling of lawsuits. Doubtless there was more to this development of great monarchic institutions than a pure and simple juridical edifice. But such was the language of power, the representation it gave of itself, and the entire theory of public law that was constructed in the Middle Ages, or reconstructed from Roman law, bears witness to the fact. Law was not simply a weapon skillfully wielded by monarchs; it was the monarchic system's mode of manifestation and the form of its acceptability. In Western societies since the Middle Ages, the exercise of power has always been formulated in terms of law.

A tradition dating back to the eighteenth or nineteenth century has accustomed us to place absolute monarchic power on the side of the unlawful: arbitrariness, abuse, caprice, willfulness, privileges and exceptions, the traditional continuance of accomplished facts. But this is to overlook a fundamental historical trait of Western monarchies: they were constructed as systems of law, they expressed themselves through theories of law, and they made their mechanisms of power work in the form of law. The old reproach that Boulainvilliers directed at the French monarchy—that it used the law and jurists to do away with rights and to bring down the aristocracy—was basically warranted by the facts. Through the development of the monarchy and its institutions this juridico-political dimension was established. It is by no means adequate to describe the manner in which power was and is exercised, but it is the code according to which power presents itself and prescribes that we conceive of it. The history of the monarchy went hand in hand with the covering up of the facts and procedures of power by juridico-political discourse.

Yet, despite the efforts that were made to disengage the juridical sphere from the monarchic institution and to free the political from the juridical, the representation of power remained caught within this system. Consider the two following examples. Criticism of the eighteenth-century monarchic institution in France was not directed against the juridico-monarchic sphere as such, but was made on behalf of a pure and rigorous juridical system to which all the mechanisms of power could conform, with no excesses or irregularities, as opposed to a monarchy which, notwithstanding its own assertions, continuously overstepped the legal framework and set itself above the laws. Political criticism availed itself, therefore, of all the juridical thinking that had accompanied the development of the monarchy, in order to condemn the latter; but it did not challenge the principle which held that law had to be the very form of power, and that power always had to be exercised in the form of law. Another type of criticism of political institutions appeared in the nineteenth century, a much more radical criticism in that it was concerned to show not only that real power escaped the rules of jurisprudence, but that the legal system itself was merely a way of exerting violence, of appropriating that violence for the benefit of the few, and of exploiting the dissymmetries and injustices of domination under cover of general law. But this critique of law is still carried out on the assumption that, ideally and by nature, power must be exercised in accordance with a fundamental lawfulness.

At bottom, despite the differences in epochs and objectives, the representation of power has remained under the spell of monarchy. In political thought and analysis, we still have not cut off the head of the king. Hence the importance that the theory of power gives to the problem of right and violence, law and illegality, freedom and will, and especially the state and sovereignty (even if the latter is questioned insofar as it is personified in a collective being and no longer a sovereign individual). To conceive of power on the basis of these problems is to conceive of it in terms of a historical form that is characteristic of our societies: the juridical monarchy. Characteristic yet transitory. For while many of its forms have persisted to the present, it has gradually been penetrated by quite new mechanisms of power that are probably irreducible to the representation of law. As we shall see, these power mechanisms are, at least in part, those that, beginning in the eighteenth century, took charge of men's existence, men as living bodies. And if it is true that the juridical system was useful for representing, albeit in a nonexhaustive way, a power that was centered primarily around deduction (*prélèvement*) and death, it is utterly incongruous with the new methods of power whose operation is not ensured by right but by technique, not by law but by normalization, not by punishment but by control, methods that are employed on all levels and in forms that go beyond the state and its apparatus. We have been engaged for centuries in a type of society in which the juridical is increasingly incapable of coding power, of serving as its system of representation. Our historical gradient carries us further and further away from a reign of law that had already begun to recede into the past at a time when the French Revolution and the accompanying age of constitutions and codes seemed to destine it for a future that was at hand.

It is this juridical representation that is still at work in recent analyses concerning the relationships of power to sex. But the problem is not to know whether desire is alien to power, whether it is prior to the law as is often thought to be the case, when it is not rather the law that is perceived as constituting it. This question is beside the point. Whether desire is this or that, in any case one continues to conceive of it in relation to a power that is always juridical and discursive, a power that has its central point in the enunciation of the law. One remains attached to a certain image of power-law, of power-sovereignty, which was traced out by the theoreticians of right and the monarchic institution. It is this image that we must break free of, that is, of the theoretical privilege of law and sovereignty, if we wish to analyze power within the concrete and historical framework of its operation. We must construct an analytics of power that no longer takes law as a model and a code.

This history of sexuality, or rather this series of studies concerning the historical relationships of power and the discourse on sex, is, I realize, a circular project in the sense that it involves two endeavors that refer back to one another. We shall try to rid ourselves of a juridical and negative representation of power, and cease to conceive of it in terms of law, prohibition, liberty, and sovereignty. But how then do we analyze what has occurred in recent history with regard to this thing—seemingly one of the most forbidden areas of our lives and bodies—that is sex? How, if not by way of prohibition and blockage, does power gain access to it? Through which mechanisms, or tactics, or devices? But let us assume in turn that a somewhat careful scrutiny will show that power in modern societies has not in fact governed sexuality through law and sovereignty; let us suppose that historical analysis has revealed the presence of a veritable "technology" of sex, one that is much more complex and above all much more positive than the mere effect of a "defense" could be; this being the case, does this example—which can only be considered a privileged one, since power seemed in this instance, more than anywhere else, to function as prohibition—not compel one to discover principles for analyzing power which do not derive from the system of right and the form of law? Hence it is a question of forming a different grid of historical decipherment by starting from a different theory of power; and, at the same time, of advancing little by little toward a different conception of power through a closer examination of an entire historical material. We must at the same time conceive of sex without the law, and power without the king.

2

Method

Hence the objective is to analyze a certain form of knowledge regarding sex, not in terms of repression or law, but in terms of power. But the word *power* is apt to lead to a number of misunderstandings—misunderstandings with respect to its nature, its form, and its unity. By power, I do not mean "Power" as a group of institutions and mechanisms that ensure the subservience of the citizens of a given state. By power, I do not mean, either, a mode of subjugation which, in contrast to violence, has the form of the rule. Finally, I do not have in mind a general system of domination exerted by one group over another, a system whose effects, through successive derivations, pervade the entire social body. The analysis, made in terms of power, must not assume that the sovereignty of the state, the form of the law, or the over-all unity of a domination are given at the outset; rather, these are only the terminal forms power takes. It seems to me that power must be understood in the first instance as the multiplicity of force relations immanent in the sphere in which they operate and which constitute their own organization; as the process which, through ceaseless struggles and confrontations, transforms, strengthens, or reverses them; as the support which these force relations find in one another, thus forming a chain or a system, or on the contrary, the disjunctions and contradictions which isolate them from one another; and lastly, as the strategies in which they take effect, whose general design or institutional crystallization is embodied in the state apparatus, in the formulation of the law, in the various social hegemonies. Power's condition of possibility, or in any case the viewpoint which permits one to understand its exercise, even in its more "peripheral" effects, and which also makes it possible to use its mechanisms as a grid of intelligibility of the social order, must not be sought in the primary existence of a central point, in a unique source of sovereignty from which secondary and descendent forms would emanate; it is the moving substrate of force relations which, by virtue of their inequality, constantly engender states of power, but the latter are always local and unstable. The omnipresence of power: not because it has the privilege of consolidating everything under its invincible unity, but because it is produced from one moment to the next, at every point, or rather in every relation from one point to another. Power is everywhere; not because it embraces everything, but because it comes from everywhere. And "Power," insofar as it is permanent, repetitious, inert, and self-reproducing, is simply the over-all effect that emerges from all these mobilities, the concatenation that rests on each of them and seeks in turn to arrest their movement. One needs to be nominalistic, no doubt: power is not an institution, and not a structure; neither is it a certain strength we are endowed with; it is the name that one attributes to a complex strategical situation in a particular society.

Should we turn the expression around, then, and say that politics is war pursued by other means? If we still wish to maintain a separation between war and politics, perhaps we should postulate rather that this multiplicity of force relations can be coded—in part but never totally—either in the form of "war," or in the form of "politics"; this would imply two different strategies (but the one always liable to switch into the other) for integrating these unbalanced, heterogeneous, unstable, and tense force relations.

Continuing this line of discussion, we can advance a certain number of propositions:

—Power is not something that is acquired, seized, or shared, something that one holds on to or allows to slip away; power is exercised from innumerable points, in the interplay of nonegalitarian and mobile relations.

—Relations of power are not in a position of exteriority with respect to other types of relationships (economic processes, knowledge relationships, sexual relations), but are immanent in the latter; they are the immediate effects of the divisions, inequalities, and disequilibriums which occur in the latter, and conversely they are the internal conditions of these differentiations; relations of power are not in superstructural positions, with merely a role of prohibition or accompaniment; they have a directly productive role, wherever they come into play.

—Power comes from below; that is, there is no binary and all-encompassing opposition between rulers and ruled at the root of power relations, and serving as a general matrix —no such duality extending from the top down and reacting on more and more limited groups to the very depths of the social body. One must suppose rather that the manifold relationships of force that take shape and come into play in the machinery of production, in families, limited groups, and institutions, are the basis for wide-ranging effects of cleavage that run through the social body as a whole. These then form a general line of force that traverses the local oppositions and links them together; to be sure, they also bring about redistributions, realignments, homogenizations, serial arrangements, and convergences of the force relations. Major dominations are the hegemonic effects that are sustained by all these confrontations.

—Power relations are both intentional and nonsubjective. If in fact they are intelligible, this is not because they are the effect of another instance that "explains" them, but rather because they are imbued, through and through, with calculation: there is no power that is exercised without a series of aims and objectives. But this does not mean that it results from the choice or decision of an individual subject; let us not look for the headquarters that presides over its rationality; neither the caste which governs, nor the groups which control the state apparatus, nor those who make the most important economic decisions direct the entire network of power that functions in a society (and makes *it* function); the rationality of power is characterized by tactics that are often quite explicit at the restricted level where they are inscribed (the local cynicism of power), tactics which, becoming connected to one another, attracting and propagating one another, but finding their base of support and their condition elsewhere, end by forming comprehensive systems: the logic is perfectly clear, the aims decipherable, and yet it is often the case that no one is there to have invented them, and few who can be said to have formulated them: an implicit characteristic of the great anonymous, almost unspoken strategies which coordinate the loquacious tactics whose "inventors" or decisionmakers are often without hypocrisy.

—Where there is power, there is resistance, and yet, or rather consequently, this resistance is never in a position of exteriority in relation to power. Should it be said that one is always "inside" power, there is no "escaping" it, there is no absolute outside where it is concerned, because one is subject to the law in any case? Or that, history being the ruse of reason, power is the ruse of history, always emerging the winner? This would be to misunderstand the strictly relational character of power relationships. Their existence depends on a multiplicity of points of resistance: these play the role of adversary, target, support, or handle in power relations. These points of resistance are present everywhere in the power network. Hence there is no single locus of great Refusal, no soul of revolt, source of all rebellions, or pure law of the revolutionary. Instead there is a plurality of resistances, each of them a special case: resistances that are possible, necessary, improbable; others that are spontaneous, savage, solitary, concerted, rampant, or violent; still others that are quick to compromise, interested, or sacrificial; by definition, they can only exist in the strategic field of power relations. But this does not mean that they are only a reaction or rebound, forming with respect to the basic domination an underside that is in the end always passive, doomed to perpetual defeat. Resistances do not derive from a few heterogeneous principles; but neither are they a lure or a promise that is of necessity betrayed. They are the odd term in relations of power; they are inscribed in the latter as an irreducible opposite. Hence they too are distributed in irregular fashion: the points, knots, or focuses of resistance are spread over time and space at varying densities, at times mobilizing groups or individuals in a definitive way, inflaming certain points of the body, certain moments in life, certain types of behavior. Are there no great radical ruptures, massive binary divisions, then? Occasionally, yes. But more often one is dealing with mobile and transitory points of resistance, producing cleavages in a society that shift about, fracturing unities and effecting regroupings, furrowing across individuals themselves, cutting them up and remolding them, marking off irreducible regions in them, in their bodies and minds. Just as the network of power relations ends by forming a dense web that passes through apparatuses and institutions, without being exactly localized in them, so too the swarm of points of resistance traverses social stratifications and individual unities. And it is doubtless the strategic codification of these points of resistance that makes a revolution possible, somewhat similar to the way in which the state relies on the institutional integration of power relationships.

It is in this sphere of force relations that we must try to analyze the mechanisms of power. In this way we will escape from the system of Law-and-Sovereign which has captivated political thought for such a long time. And if it is true that Machiavelli was among the few—and this no doubt was the scandal of his "cynicism"—who conceived the power of the Prince in terms of <u>force</u> relationships, perhaps we need to go one step further, do without the persona of the Prince, and decipher power mechanisms on the basis of a strategy that is immanent in force relationships.

To return to sex and the discourses of truth that have taken charge of it, the question that we must address, then, is not: Given a specific state structure, how and why is it that power needs to establish a knowledge of sex? Neither is the question: What over-all domination was served by the concern, evidenced since the eighteenth century, to produce true discourses on sex? Nor is it: What law presided over both the regularity of sexual behavior and the conformity of what was said about it? It is rather: In a specific type of discourse on sex, in a specific form of extortion of truth, appearing historically and in specific places (around the child's body, apropos of women's sex, in connection with practices restricting births, and so on), <u>what were the most immediate, the most local power relations at work</u>? How did they make possible these kinds of discourses, and conversely, how were these discourses used to support power relations? How was the action of these power relations modified by their very exercise, entailing a strengthening of some terms and a weakening of others, with effects of resistance and counterinvestments, so that there has never existed one type of stable subjugation, given once and for all? How were these power relations linked to one another according to the logic of a great strategy, which in retrospect takes on the aspect of a unitary and voluntarist politics of sex? In general terms: rather than referring all the infinitesimal violences that are exerted on sex, all the anxious gazes that are directed at it, and all the hiding places whose discovery is made into an impossible task, to the unique form of a great Power, we must immerse the expanding production of discourses on sex in the field of multiple and mobile power relations.

Which leads us to advance, in a preliminary way, four rules to follow. But these are not intended as methodological imperatives; at most they are cautionary prescriptions.

1. *Rule of immanence*

One must not suppose that there exists a certain sphere of sexuality that would be the legitimate concern of a free and disinterested scientific inquiry were it not the object of mechanisms of prohibition brought to bear by the economic or ideological requirements of power. If sexuality was constituted as an area of investigation, this was only because relations of power had established it as a possible object; and conversely, if power was able to take it as a target, this was because techniques of knowledge and procedures of discourse were capable of investing it. Between techniques of knowledge and strategies of power, there is no exteriority, even if they have specific roles and are linked together on the basis of their difference. We will start, therefore, from what might be called "local centers" of power-knowledge: for example, the relations that obtain between penitents and confessors, or the faithful and their directors of conscience. Here, guided by the theme of the "flesh" that must be mastered, different forms of discourse—self-examination, questionings, admissions, interpretations, interviews—were the vehicle of a kind of incessant back-and-forth movement of forms of subjugation and schemas of knowledge. Similarly, the body of the child, under surveillance, surrounded in his cradle, his bed, or his room by an entire watch-crew of parents, nurses, servants, educators, and doctors, all attentive to the least manifestations of his sex, has constituted, particularly since the eighteenth century, another "local center" of power-knowledge.

2. *Rules of continual variations*

We must not look for who has the power in the order of sexuality (men, adults, parents, doctors) and who is deprived of it (women, adolescents, children, patients); nor for who has the right to know and who is forced to remain ignorant. We must seek rather the pattern of the modifications which the relationships of force imply by the very nature of their process. The "distributions of power" and the "appropriations of knowledge" never represent only instantaneous slices taken from processes involving, for example, a cumulative reinforcement of the strongest factor, or a reversal of relationship, or again, a simultaneous increase of two terms. Relations of power-knowledge are not static forms of distribution, they are "matrices of transformations." The nineteenth-century grouping made up of the father, the mother, the educator, and the doctor, around the child and his sex, was subjected to constant modifications, continual shifts. One of the more spectacular results of the latter was a strange reversal: whereas to begin with the child's sexuality had been problematized within the relationship established between doctor and parents (in the form of advice, or recommendations to keep the child under observation, or warnings of future dangers), ultimately it was in the relationship of the psychiatrist to the child that the sexuality of adults themselves was called into question.

3. *Rule of double conditioning*

No "local center," no "pattern of transformation" could function if, through a series of sequences, it did not eventually enter into an over-all strategy. And inversely, no strategy could achieve comprehensive effects if did not gain support from precise and tenuous relations serving, not as its point of application or final outcome, but as its prop and anchor point. There is no discontinuity between them, as if one were dealing with two different levels (one microscopic and the other macroscopic); but neither is there homogeneity (as if the one were only the enlarged projection or the miniaturization of the other); rather, one must conceive of the double conditioning of a strategy by the specificity of possible tactics, and of tactics by the strategic envelope that makes them work. Thus the father in the family is not the "representative" of the sovereign or the state; and the latter are not projections of the father on a different scale. The family does not duplicate society, just as society does not imitate the family. But the family organization, precisely to the extent that it was insular and heteromorphous with respect to the other power mechanisms, was used to support the great "maneuvers" employed for the Malthusian control of the birthrate, for the populationist incitements, for the medicalization of sex and the psychiatrization of its nongenital forms.

4. *Rule of the tactical polyvalence of discourses*

What is said about sex must not be analyzed simply as the surface of projection of these power mechanisms. Indeed, it is in discourse that power and knowledge are joined together. And for this very reason, we must conceive discourse as a series of discontinuous segments whose tactical function is neither uniform nor stable. To be more precise, we must not imagine a world of discourse divided between accepted discourse and excluded discourse, or between the dominant discourse and the dominated one; but as a multiplicity of discursive elements that can come into play in various strategies. It is this distribution that we must reconstruct, with the things said and those concealed, the enunciations required and those forbidden, that it comprises; with the variants and different effects—according to who is speaking, his position of power, the institutional context in which he happens to be situated—that it implies; and with the shifts and reutilizations of identical formulas for contrary objectives that it also includes. Discourses are not once and for all subservient to power or raised up against it, any more than silences are. We must make allowance for the complex and unstable process whereby discourse can be both an instrument and an effect of power, but also a hindrance, a stumbling-block, a point of resistance and a starting point for an opposing strategy. Discourse transmits and produces power; it reinforces it, but also undermines and exposes it, renders it fragile and makes it possible to thwart it. In like manner, silence and secrecy are a shelter for power, anchoring its prohibitions; but they also loosen its holds and provide for relatively obscure areas of tolerance. Consider for example the history of what was once "the" great sin against nature. The extreme discretion of the texts dealing with sodomy—that utterly confused category—and the nearly universal reticence in talking about it made possible a twofold operation: on the one hand, there was an extreme severity (punishment by fire was meted out well into the eighteenth century, without there being any substantial protest expressed before the middle of the century), and on the other hand, a tolerance that must have been widespread (which one can deduce indirectly from the infrequency of judicial sentences, and which one glimpses more directly through certain statements concerning societies of men that were thought to exist in the army or in the courts). There is no question that the appearance in nineteenth-century psychiatry, jurisprudence, and literature of a whole series of discourses on the species and subspecies of homosexuality, inversion, pederasty, and "psychic hermaphrodism" made possible a strong advance of social controls into this area of "perversity"; but it also made possible the formation of a "reverse" discourse: homosexuality began to speak in its own behalf, to demand that its legitimacy or "naturality" be acknowledged, often in the same vocabulary, using the same categories by which it was medically disqualified. There is not, on the one side, a discourse of power, and opposite it, another discourse that runs counter to it. Discourses are tactical elements or blocks operating in the field of force relations; there can exist different and even contradictory discourses within the same strategy; they can, on the contrary, circulate without changing their form from one strategy to another, opposing strategy. We must not expect the discourses on sex to tell us, above all, what strategy they derive from, or what moral divisions they accompany, or what ideology—dominant or dominated—they represent; rather we must question them on the two levels of their tactical productivity (what reciprocal effects of power and knowledge they ensure) and their strategical integration (what conjunction and what force relationship make their utilization necessary in a given episode of the various confrontations that occur).

In short, it is a question of orienting ourselves to a conception of power which replaces the privilege of the law with the viewpoint of the objective, the privilege of prohibition with the viewpoint of tactical efficacy, the privilege of sovereignty with the analysis of a multiple and mobile field of force relations, wherein far-reaching, but never completely stable, effects of domination are produced. The strategical model, rather than the model based on law. And this, not out of a speculative choice or theoretical preference, but because in fact it is one of the essential traits of Western societies that the force relationships which for a long time had found expression in war, in every form of warfare, gradually became invested in the order of political power.

3

Domain

Sexuality must not be described as a stubborn drive, by nature alien and of necessity disobedient to a power which exhausts itself trying to subdue it and often fails to control it entirely. It appears rather as an especially dense transfer point for relations of power: between men and women, young people and old people, parents and offspring, teachers and students, priests and laity, an administration and a population. Sexuality is not the most intractable element in power relations, but rather one of those endowed with the greatest instrumentality: useful for the greatest number of maneuvers and capable of serving as a point of support, as a linchpin, for the most varied strategies.

There is no single, all-encompassing strategy, valid for all of society and uniformly bearing on all the manifestations of sex. For example, the idea that there have been repeated attempts, by various means, to reduce all of sex to its reproductive function, its heterosexual and adult form, and its matrimonial legitimacy fails to take into account the manifold objectives aimed for, the manifold means employed in the different sexual politics concerned with the two sexes, the different age groups and social classes.

In a first approach to the problem, it seems that we can distinguish four great strategic unities which, beginning in the eighteenth century, formed specific mechanisms of knowledge and power centering on sex. These did not come into being fully developed at that time; but it was then that they took on a consistency and gained an effectiveness in the order of power, as well as a productivity in the order of knowledge, so that it is possible to describe them in their relative autonomy.

1. *A hysterization of women's bodies:* a threefold process whereby the feminine body was analyzed—qualified and disqualified—as being thoroughly saturated with sexuality; whereby it was integrated into the sphere of medical practices, by reason of a pathology intrinsic to it; whereby, finally, it was placed in organic communication with the social body (whose regulated fecundity it was supposed to ensure), the family space (of which it had to be a substantial and functional element), and the life of children (which it produced and had to guarantee, by virtue of a biologico-moral responsibility lasting through the entire period of the children's education): the Mother, with her negative image of "nervous woman," constituted the most visible form of this hysterization.

2. *A pedagogization of children's sex:* a double assertion that practically all children indulge or are prone to indulge in sexual activity; and that, being unwarranted, at the same time "natural" and "contrary to nature," this sexual activity posed physical and moral, individual and collective dangers; children were defined as "preliminary" sexual beings, on this side of sex, yet within it, astride a dangerous dividing line. Parents, families, educators, doctors, and eventually psychologists would have to take charge, in a continuous way, of this precious and perilous, dangerous and endangered sexual potential: this pedagogization was especially evident in the war against onanism, which in the West lasted nearly two centuries.

3. *A socialization of procreative behavior:* an economic socialization via all the incitements and restrictions, the "social" and fiscal measures brought to bear on the fertility of

couples; a political socialization achieved through the "responsibilization" of couples with regard to the social body as a whole (which had to be limited or on the contrary reinvigorated), and a medical socialization carried out by attributing a pathogenic value—for the individual and the species—to birth-control practices.

4. *A psychiatrization of perverse pleasure:* the sexual instinct was isolated as a separate biological and psychical instinct; a clinical analysis was made of all the forms of anomalies by which it could be afflicted; it was assigned a role of normalization or pathologization with respect to all behavior; and finally, a corrective technology was sought for these anomalies.

Four figures emerged from this preoccupation with sex, which mounted throughout the nineteenth century—four privileged objects of knowledge, which were also targets and anchorage points for the ventures of knowledge: the hysterical woman, the masturbating child, the Malthusian couple, and the perverse adult. Each of them corresponded to one of these strategies which, each in its own way, invested and made use of the sex of women, children, and men.

What was at issue in these strategies? A struggle against sexuality? Or were they part of an effort to gain control of it? An attempt to regulate it more effectively and mask its more indiscreet, conspicuous, and intractable aspects? A way of formulating only that measure of knowledge about it that was acceptable or useful? In actual fact, what was involved, rather, was the very production of sexuality. Sexuality must not be thought of as a kind of natural given which power tries to hold in check, or as an obscure domain which knowledge tries gradually to uncover. It is the name that can be given to a historical construct: not a furtive reality that is difficult to grasp, but a great surface network in which the stimulation of bodies, the intensification of pleasures, the incitement to discourse, the formation of special knowledges, the strengthening of controls and resistances, are linked to one another, in accordance with a few major strategies of knowledge and power.

It will be granted no doubt that relations of sex gave rise, in every society, to a *deployment of alliance:* a system of marriage, of fixation and development of kinship ties, of transmission of names and possessions. This deployment of alliance, with the mechanisms of constraint that ensured its existence and the complex knowledge it often required, lost some of its importance as economic processes and political structures could no longer rely on it as an adequate instrument or sufficient support. Particularly from the eighteenth century onward, Western societies created and deployed a new apparatus which was superimposed on the previous one, and which, without completely supplanting the latter, helped to reduce its importance. I am speaking of the *deployment of sexuality:* like the *deployment of alliance,* it connects up with the circuit of sexual partners, but in a completely different way. The two systems can be contrasted term by term. The deployment of alliance is built around a system of rules defining the permitted and the forbidden, the licit and the illicit, whereas the deployment of sexuality operates according to mobile, polymorphous, and contingent techniques of power. The deployment of alliance has as one of its chief objectives to reproduce the interplay of relations and maintain the law that governs them; the deployment of sexuality, on the other hand, engenders a continual extension of areas and forms of control. For the first, what is pertinent is the link between partners and definite statutes; the second is concerned with the sensations of the body, the quality of pleasures, and the nature of impressions, however tenuous or imperceptible these may be. Lastly, if the deployment of alliance is firmly tied to the economy due to the role it can play in the transmission or circulation of wealth, the deployment of sexuality is linked to the economy through numerous and subtle relays, the main one of which, however, is the body—the body that produces and consumes. In a word, the deployment of alliance is attuned to a homeostasis of the social body, which it has the function of maintaining; whence its privileged link with the law; whence too the fact that the important phase for it is "reproduction." The deployment of sexuality has its reason for being, not in reproducing itself, but in proliferating, innovating, annexing, creating, and penetrating bodies in an increasingly detailed way, and in controlling populations in an increasingly comprehensive way. We are compelled, then, to accept three or four hypotheses which run counter to the one on which the theme of a sexuality repressed by the modern forms of society is based: sexuality is tied to recent devices of power; it has been expanding at an increasing rate since the seventeenth century; the arrangement that has sustained it is not governed by reproduction; it has been linked from the outset with an intensification of the body—with its exploitation as an object of knowledge and an element in relations of power.

It is not exact to say that the deployment of sexuality supplanted the deployment of alliance. One can imagine that one day it will have replaced it. But as things stand at present, while it does tend to cover up the deployment of alliance, it has neither obliterated the latter nor rendered it useless. Moreover, historically it was around and on the basis of the deployment of alliance that the deployment of sexuality was constructed. First the practice of penance, then that of the examination of conscience and spiritual direction, was the formative nucleus: as we have seen,[1] what was at issue to begin with at the tribunal of penance was sex insofar as it was the basis of relations; the questions posed had to do with the commerce allowed or forbidden (adultery, extramarital relations, relations with a person prohibited by blood or statute, the legitimate or illegitimate character of the act of sexual

[1] Cf page 37 above.

congress); then, coinciding with the new pastoral and its application in seminaries, secondary schools, and convents, there was a gradual progression away from the problematic of relations toward a problematic of the "flesh," that is, of the body, sensation, the nature of pleasure, the more secret forms of enjoyment or acquiescence. "Sexuality" was taking shape, born of a technology of power that was originally focused on alliance. Since then, it has not ceased to operate in conjunction with a system of alliance on which it has depended for support. The family cell, in the form in which it came to be valued in the course of the eighteenth century, made it possible for the main elements of the deployment of sexuality (the feminine body, infantile precocity, the regulation of births, and to a lesser extent no doubt, the specification of the perverted) to develop along its two primary dimensions: the husband-wife axis and the parents-children axis. The family, in its contemporary form, must not be understood as a social, economic, and political structure of alliance that excludes or at least restrains sexuality, that diminishes it as much as possible, preserving only its useful functions. On the contrary, its role is to anchor sexuality and provide it with a permanent support. It ensures the production of a sexuality that is not homogeneous with the privileges of alliance, while making it possible for the systems of alliance to be imbued with a new tactic of power which they would otherwise be impervious to. The family is the interchange of sexuality and alliance: it conveys the law and the juridical dimension in the deployment of sexuality; and it conveys the economy of pleasure and the intensity of sensations in the regime of alliance.

This interpenetration of the deployment of alliance and that of sexuality in the form of the family allows us to understand a number of facts: that since the eighteenth century the family has become an obligatory locus of affects, feelings, love; that sexuality has its privileged point of development in the family; that for this reason sexuality is "incestuous" from the start. It may be that in societies where the mechanisms of alliance predominate, prohibition of incest is a functionally indispensable rule. But in a society such as ours, where the family is the most active site of sexuality, and where it is doubtless the exigencies of the latter which maintain and prolong its existence, incest—for different reasons altogether and in a completely different way—occupies a central place; it is constantly being solicited and refused; it is an object of obsession and attraction, a dreadful secret and an indispensable pivot. It is manifested as a thing that is strictly forbidden in the family insofar as the latter functions as a deployment of alliance; but it is also a thing that is continuously demanded in order for the family to be a hotbed of constant sexual incitement. If for more than a century the West has displayed such a strong interest in the prohibition of incest, if more or less by common accord it has been seen as a social universal and one of the points through which every society is obliged to pass on the way to becoming a culture, perhaps this is because it was found to be a means of self-defense, not against an incestuous desire, but against the expansion and the implications of this deployment of sexuality which had been set up, but which, among its its many benefits, had the disadvantage of ignoring the laws and juridical forms of alliance. By asserting that all societies without exception, and consequently our own, were subject to this rule of rules, one guaranteed that this deployment of sexuality, whose strange effects were beginning to be felt—among them, the affective intensification of the family space—would not be able to escape from the grand and ancient system of alliance. Thus the law would be secure, even in the new mechanics of power. For this is the paradox of a society which, from the eighteenth century to the present, has created so many technologies of power that are foreign to the concept of law: it fears the effects and proliferations of those technologies and attempts to recode them in forms of law. If one considers the threshold of all culture to be prohibited incest, then sexuality has been, from the dawn of time, under the sway of law and right. By devoting so much effort to an endless reworking of the transcultural theory of the incest taboo, anthropology has proved worthy of the whole modern deployment of sexuality and the theoretical discourses it generates.

What has taken place since the seventeenth century can be interpreted in the following manner: the deployment of sexuality which first developed on the fringes of familial institutions (in the direction of conscience and pedagogy, for example) gradually became focused on the family: the alien, irreducible, and even perilous effects it held in store for the deployment of alliance (an awareness of this danger was evidenced in the criticism often directed at the indiscretion of the directors, and in the entire controversy, which occurred somewhat later, over the private or public, institutional or familial education of children[2]) were absorbed by the family, a family that was reorganized, restricted no doubt, and in any case intensified in comparison with the functions it formerly exercised in the deployment of alliance. In the family, parents and relatives became the chief agents of a deployment of sexuality which drew its outside support from doctors, educators, and later psychiatrists, and which began by competing with the relations of alliance but soon "psychologized" or "psychiatrized" the latter. Then these new personages made their appearance: the nervous woman, the frigid wife, the indifferent mother—or worse, the mother beset by murderous obsessions—the impotent, sadistic, perverse husband, the hysterical or neurasthenic girl, the precocious and already exhausted child, and the young homosexual who rejects marriage or neglects his wife. These were the combined figures of an alliance gone bad and an abnormal sexuality; they were the means by which the disturbing factors of the latter were brought into the former;

[2] Molière's *Tartuffe* and Jakob Michael Lenz's *Tutor*, separated by more than a century, both depict the interference of the deployment of sexuality in the family organization, apropos of spiritual direction in *Tartuffe* and education in *The Tutor*.

and yet they also provided an opportunity for the alliance system to assert its prerogatives in the order of sexuality. Then a pressing demand emanated from the family: a plea for help in reconciling these unfortunate conflicts between sexuality and alliance; and, caught in the grip of this deployment of sexuality which had invested it from without, contributing to its solidification into its modern form, the family broadcast the long complaint of its sexual suffering to doctors, educators, psychiatrists, priests, and pastors, to all the "experts" who would listen. It was as if it had suddenly discovered the dreadful secret of what had always been hinted at and inculcated in it: the family, the keystone of alliance, was the germ of all the misfortunes of sex. And lo and behold, from the mid-nineteenth century onward, the family engaged in searching out the slightest traces of sexuality in its midst, wrenching from itself the most difficult confessions, soliciting an audience with everyone who might know something about the matter, and opening itself unreservedly to endless examination. The family was the crystal in the deployment of sexuality: it seemed to be the source of a sexuality which it actually only reflected and diffracted. By virtue of its permeability, and through that process of reflections to the outside, it became one of the most valuable tactical components of the deployment.

But this development was not without its tensions and problems. Charcot doubtless constituted a central figure in this as well. For many years he was the most noteworthy of all those to whom families, burdened down as they were with this sexuality that saturated them, appealed for mediation and treatment. On receiving parents who brought him their children, husbands their wives, and wives their husbands, from the world over, his first concern was to separate the "patient" from his family, and the better to observe him, he would pay as little attention as possible to what the family had to say.[3] He sought to detach the sphere of sexuality from the system of alliance, in order to deal with it directly through a medical practice whose technicity and autonomy were guaranteed by the neurological model. Medicine thus assumed final responsibility, according to the rules of a specific knowledge, for a sexuality which it had in fact urged families to concern themselves with as an essential task and a major danger. Moreover, Charcot noted on several occasions how difficult it was for families to "yield" the patient whom they nonetheless had brought to the doctor, how they laid siege to the mental hospitals where the subject was being kept out of view, and the ways in which they were constantly interfering with the doctor's work. Their worry was unwarranted, however: the therapist only intervened in order to return to them individuals who were sexually compatible with the family system; and while this intervention manipulated the sexual body, it did not authorize the latter to define itself in explicit discourse. One must not speak of these "genital causes": so went the phrase—muttered in a muted voice —which the most famous ears of our time overheard one day in 1886, from the mouth of Charcot.

This was the context in which psychoanalysis set to work; but not without substantially modifying the pattern of anxieties and reassurances. In the beginning it must have given rise to distrust and hostility, for, pushing Charcot's lesson to the extreme, it undertook to examine the sexuality of individuals outside family control; it brought this sexuality to light without covering it over again with the neurological model; more serious still, it called family relations into question in the analysis it made of them. But despite everything,

[3] Jean-Martin Charcot, *Leçons de Mardi,* January 7, 1888: "In order to properly treat a hysterical girl, one must not leave her with her father and mother; she needs to be placed in a mental hospital. . . . Do you know how long well-behaved little girls cry for their mothers after they part company? . . . Let us take the average, if you will; it's not very long, a half-hour or thereabouts."

February 21, 1888: "In the case of hysteria of young boys, what one must do is to separate them from their mothers. So long as they are with their mothers, nothing is of any use. . . . The father is sometimes just as unbearable as the mother; it is best, then, to get rid of them both."

psychoanalysis, whose technical procedure seemed to place the confession of sexuality outside family jurisdiction, rediscovered the law of alliance, the involved workings of marriage and kinship, and incest at the heart of this sexuality, as the principle of its formation and the key to its intelligibility. The guarantee that one would find the parents-children relationship at the root of everyone's sexuality made it possible —even when everything seemed to point to the reverse process—to keep the deployment of sexuality coupled to the system of alliance. There was no risk that sexuality would appear to be, by nature, alien to the law: it was constituted only through the law. Parents, do not be afraid to bring your children to analysis: it will teach them that in any case it is you whom they love. Children, you really shouldn't complain that you are not orphans, that you always rediscover in your innermost selves your Object-Mother or the sovereign sign of your Father: it is through them that you gain access to desire. Whence, after so many reticences, the enormous consumption of analysis in societies where the deployment of alliance and the family system needed strengthening. For this is one of the most significant aspects of this entire history of the deployment of sexuality: it had its beginnings in the technology of the "flesh" in classical Christianity, basing itself on the alliance system and the rules that governed the latter; but today it fills a reverse function in that it tends to prop up the old deployment of alliance. From the direction of conscience to psychoanalysis, the deployments of alliance and sexuality were involved in a slow process that had them turning about one another until, more than three centuries later, their positions were reversed; in the Christian pastoral, the law of alliance codified the flesh which was just being discovered and fitted it into a framework that was still juridical in character; with psychoanalysis, sexuality gave body and life to the rules of alliance by saturating them with desire.

Hence the domain we must analyze in the different studies that will follow the present volume is that deployment of sexuality: its formation on the basis of the Christian notion of the flesh, and its development through the four great strategies that were deployed in the nineteenth century: the sexualization of children, the hysterization of women, the specification of the perverted, and the regulation of populations—all strategies that went by way of a family which must be viewed, not as a powerful agency of prohibition, but as a major factor of sexualization.

The first phase corresponded to the need to form a "labor force" (hence to avoid any useless "expenditure," any wasted energy, so that all forces were reduced to labor capacity alone) and to ensure its reproduction (conjugality, the regulated fabrication of children). The second phase corresponded to that epoch of *Spätkapitalismus* in which the exploitation of wage labor does not demand the same violent and physical constraints as in the nineteenth century, and where the politics of the body does not require the elision of sex or its restriction solely to the reproductive function; it relies instead on a multiple channeling into the controlled circuits of the economy—on what has been called a hyper-repressive desublimation.

If the politics of sex makes little use of the law of the taboo but brings into play an entire technical machinery, if what is involved is the production of sexuality rather than the repression of sex, then our emphasis has to be placed elsewhere; we must shift our analysis away from the problem of "labor capacity" and doubtless abandon the diffuse energetics that underlies the theme of a sexuality repressed for economic reasons.

4

Periodization

The history of sexuality supposes two ruptures if one tries to center it on mechanisms of repression. The first, occurring in the course of the seventeenth century, was characterized by the advent of the great prohibitions, the exclusive promotion of adult marital sexuality, the imperatives of decency, the obligatory concealment of the body, the reduction to silence and mandatory reticences of language. The second, a twentieth-century phenomenon, was really less a rupture than an inflexion of the curve: this was the moment when the mechanisms of repression were seen as beginning to loosen their grip; one passed from insistent sexual taboos to a relative tolerance with regard to prenuptial or extramarital relations; the disqualification of "perverts" diminished, their condemnation by the law was in part eliminated; a good many of the taboos that weighed on the sexuality of children were lifted.

We must attempt to trace the chronology of these devices: the inventions, the instrumental mutations, and the renovations of previous techniques. But there is also the calendar of their utilization to consider, the chronology of their diffusion and of the effects (of subjugation and resistance) they produced. These multiple datings doubtless will not coincide with the great repressive cycle that is ordinarily situated between the seventeenth and the twentieth centuries.

1. The chronology of the techniques themselves goes back

a long way. Their point of formation must be sought in the penitential practices of medieval Christianity, or rather in the dual series constituted by the obligatory, exhaustive, and periodic confession imposed on all the faithful by the Lateran Council and by the methods of asceticism, spiritual exercise, and mysticism that evolved with special intensity from the sixteenth century on. First the Reformation, then Tridentine Catholicism, mark an important mutation and a schism in what might be called the "traditional technology of the flesh." A division whose depth should not be underestimated; but this did not rule out a certain parallelism in the Catholic and Protestant methods of examination of conscience and pastoral direction: procedures for analyzing "concupiscence" and transforming it into discourse were established in both instances. This was a rich, refined technique which began to take shape in the sixteenth century and went through a long series of theoretical elaborations until, at the end of the eighteenth century, it became fixed in expressions capable of symbolizing the mitigated strictness of Alfonso de' Liguori in the one case and Wesleyan pedagogy in the other.

It was during the same period—the end of the eighteenth century—and for reasons that will have to be determined, that there emerged a completely new technology of sex; new in that for the most part it escaped the ecclesiastical institution without being truly independent of the thematics of sin. Through pedagogy, medicine, and economics, it made sex not only a secular concern but a concern of the state as well; to be more exact, sex became a matter that required the social body as a whole, and virtually all of its individuals, to place themselves under surveillance. New too for the fact that it expanded along three axes: that of pedagogy, having as its objective the specific sexuality of children; that of medicine, whose objective was the sexual physiology peculiar to women; and last, that of demography, whose objective was the spontaneous or concerted regulation of births. Thus the "sin of youth," "nervous disorders," and "frauds against procreation" (as those "deadly secrets" were later to be called) designate three privileged areas of this new technology. There is no question that in each of these areas, it went back to methods that had already been formed by Christianity, but of course not without modifying them: the sexuality of children was already problematized in the spiritual pedagogy of Christianity (it is interesting to note that *Mollities,* the first treatise on sin, was written in the fifteenth century by an educator and mystic named Gerson, and that the *Onania* collection compiled by Dekker in the eighteenth century repeats word for word examples set forth by the Anglican pastoral); the eighteenth-century medicine of nerves and vapors took up in turn a field of analysis that had already been delimited when the phenomena of possession fomented a grave crisis in the all too indiscreet practices of conscience direction and spiritual examination (nervous illness is certainly not the truth of possession, but the medicine of hysteria is not unrelated to the earlier direction of "obsessed" women); and the campaigns apropos of the birthrate took the place of the control of conjugal relations—in a different form and at another level—which the Christian penance had so persistently sought to establish through its examinations. A visible continuity, therefore, but one that did not prevent a major transformation: from that time on, the technology of sex was ordered in relation to the medical institution, the exigency of normality, and—instead of the question of death and everlasting punishment—the problem of life and illness. The flesh was brought down to the level of the organism.

This mutation took place at the turn of the nineteenth century; it opened the way for many other transformations that derived from it. The first of these set apart the medicine of sex from the medicine of the body; it isolated a sexual "instinct" capable of presenting constitutive anomalies, acquired derivations, infirmities, or pathological processes.

Heinrich Kaan's *Psychopathia Sexualis,* published in 1846, can be used as an indicator: these were the years that saw the correlative appearance of a medicine, an "orthopedics," specific to sex: in a word, the opening up of the great medico-psychological domain of the "perversions," which was destined to take over from the old moral categories of debauchery and excess. In the same period, the analysis of heredity was placing sex (sexual relations, venereal diseases, matrimonial alliances, perversions) in a position of "biological responsibility" with regard to the species: not only could sex be affected by its own diseases, it could also, if it was not controlled, transmit diseases or create others that would afflict future generations. Thus it appeared to be the source of an entire capital for the species to draw from. Whence the medical—but also political—project for organizing a state management of marriages, births, and life expectancies; sex and its fertility had to be administered. The medicine of perversions and the programs of eugenics were the two great innovations in the technology of sex of the second half of the nineteenth century.

Innovations that merged together quite well, for the theory of "degenerescence" made it possible for them to perpetually refer back to one another; it explained how a heredity that was burdened with various maladies (it made little difference whether these were organic, functional, or psychical) ended by producing a sexual pervert (look into the genealogy of an exhibitionist or a homosexual: you will find a hemiplegic ancestor, a phthisic parent, or an uncle afflicted with senile dementia); but it went on to explain how a sexual perversion resulted in the depletion of one's line of descent —rickets in the children, the sterility of future generations. The series composed of perversion-heredity-degenerescence formed the solid nucleus of the new technologies of sex. And let it not be imagined that this was nothing more than a medical theory which was scientifically lacking and improperly moralistic. Its application was widespread and its im-

plantation went deep. Psychiatry, to be sure, but also jurisprudence, legal medicine, agencies of social control, the surveillance of dangerous or endangered children, all functioned for a long time on the basis of "degenerescence" and the heredity-perversion system. An entire
social practice, which took the exasperated but coherent
form of a state-directed racism, furnished this technology of
sex with a formidable power and far-reaching consequences.

And the strange position of psychiatry at the end of the
nineteenth century would be hard to comprehend if one did
not see the rupture it brought about in the great system of
degenerescence: it resumed the project of a medical technology appropriate for dealing with the sexual instinct; but it
sought to free it from its ties with heredity, and hence from
eugenics and the various racisms. It is very well to look back
from our vantage point and remark upon the normalizing
impulse in Freud; one can go on to denounce the role played
for many years by the psychoanalytic institution; but the fact
remains that in the great family of technologies of sex, which
goes so far back into the history of the Christian West, of all
those institutions that set out in the nineteenth century to
medicalize sex, it was the one that, up to the decade of the
forties, rigorously opposed the political and institutional
effects of the perversion-heredity-degenerescence system.

It is clear that the genealogy of all these techniques, with
their mutations, their shifts, their continuities and ruptures,
does not coincide with the hypothesis of a great repressive
phase that was inaugurated in the course of the classical age
and began to slowly decline in the twentieth. There was
rather a perpetual inventiveness, a steady growth of methods
and procedures, with two especially productive moments in
this proliferating history: around the middle of the sixteenth
century, the development of procedures of direction and
examination of conscience; and at the beginning of the nineteenth century, the advent of medical technologies of sex.

2. But the foregoing is still only a dating of the techniques

themselves. The history of their spread and their point of application is something else again. If one writes the history of sexuality in terms of repression, relating this repression to the utilization of labor capacity, one must suppose that sexual controls were the more intense and meticulous as they were directed at the poorer classes; one has to assume that they followed the path of greatest domination and the most systematic exploitation: the young adult man, possessing nothing more than his life force, had to be the primary target of a subjugation destined to shift the energy available for useless pleasure toward compulsory labor. But this does not appear to be the way things actually happened. On the contrary, the most rigorous techniques were formed and, more particularly, applied first, with the greatest intensity, in the economically privileged and politically dominant classes. The direction of consciences, self-examination, the entire long elaboration of the transgressions of the flesh, and the scrupulous detection of concupiscence were all subtle procedures that could only have been accessible to small groups of people. It is true that the penitential method of Alfonso de' Liguori and the rules recommended to the Methodists by Wesley ensured that these procedures would be more widely disseminated, after a fashion; but this was at the cost of a considerable simplification.

The same can be said of the family as an agency of control and a point of sexual saturation: it was in the "bourgeois" or "aristocratic" family that the sexuality of children and adolescents was first problematized, and feminine sexuality medicalized; it was the first to be alerted to the potential pathology of sex, the urgent need to keep it under close watch and to devise a rational technology of correction. It was this family that first became a locus for the psychiatrization of sex. Surrendering to fears, creating remedies, appealing for rescue by learned techniques, generating countless discourses, it was the first to commit itself to sexual erethism. The bourgeoisie began by considering that its own sex was something important, a fragile treasure, a secret that had to be discovered at all costs. It is worth remembering that the first figure to be invested by the deployment of sexuality, one of the first to be "sexualized," was the "idle" woman. She inhabited the outer edge of the "world," in which she always had to appear as a value, and of the family, where she was assigned a new destiny charged with conjugal and parental obligations. Thus there emerged the "nervous" woman, the woman afflicted with "vapors"; in this figure, the hysterization of woman found its anchorage point. As for the adolescent wasting his future substance in secret pleasures, the onanistic child who was of such concern to doctors and educators from the end of the eighteenth century to the end of the nineteenth, this was not the child of the people, the future worker who had to be taught the disciplines of the body, but rather the schoolboy, the child surrounded by domestic servants, tutors, and governesses, who was in danger of compromising not so much his physical strength as his intellectual capacity, his moral fiber, and the obligation to preserve a healthy line of descent for his family and his social class.

For their part, the working classes managed for a long time to escape the deployment of "sexuality. " Of course, they were subjected in specific ways to the deployment of "alliances": the exploitation of legitimate marriage and fertility, the exclusion of consanguine sexual union, prescriptions of social and local endogamy. On the other hand, it is unlikely that the Christian technology of the flesh ever had any importance for them. As for the mechanisms of sexualization, these penetrated them slowly and apparently in three successive stages. The first involved the problems of birth control, when it was discovered, at the end of the eighteenth century, that the art of fooling nature was not the exclusive privilege of city dwellers and libertines, but was known and practiced by those who, being close to nature itself, should have held it to be more repugnant than anyone else did. Next the organization of the "conventional" family came to be regarded, sometime around the eighteen-thirties, as an indispensable instrument of political control and economic regulation for the subjugation of the urban proletariat: there was a great campaign for the "moralization of the poorer classes." The last stage came at the end of the nineteenth century with the development of the juridical and medical control of perversions, for the sake of a general protection of society and the race. It can be said that this was the moment when the deployment of "sexuality," elaborated in its more complex and intense forms, by and for the privileged classes, spread through the entire social body. But the forms it took were not everywhere the same, and neither were the instruments it employed (the respective roles of medical and judicial authority were not the same in both instances; nor was even the way in which medicine and sexuality functioned).

These chronological reminders—whether we are concerned with the invention of techniques or the calendar of their diffusion—are of some importance. They cast much doubt on the idea of a repressive cycle, with a beginning and an end and forming a curve with its point of inflexion: it appears unlikely that there was an age of sexual restriction. They also make it doubtful that the process' was homogeneous at all levels of society and in all social classes: there was no unitary sexual politics. But above all, they make the meaning of the process, and its reasons for being, problematical: it seems that the deployment of sexuality was not established as a principle of limitation of the pleasures of others by what have traditionally been called the "ruling classes." Rather it appears to me that they first tried it on themselves. Was this a new avatar of that bourgeois asceticism described so many times in connection with the Reformation, the new work ethic, and the rise of capitalism? It seems in fact that what was involved was not an asceticism, in any case not a renunciation of pleasure or a disqualification of the flesh, but on the contrary an intensification of the body, a problematization of health and its operational terms: it was a question of techniques for maximizing life. The primary concern was not repression of the sex of the classes to be exploited, but rather the body, vigor, longevity, progeniture, and descent of the classes that "ruled." This was the purpose for which the deployment of sexuality was first established, as a new distribution of pleasures, discourses, truths, and powers; it has to be seen as the self-affirmation of one class rather than the enslavement of another: a defense, a protection, a strengthening, and an exaltation that were eventually extended to others—at the cost of different transformations—as a means of social control and political subjugation. With this investment of its own sex by a technology of power and knowledge which it had itself invented, the bourgeoisie underscored the high political price of its body, sensations, and pleasures, its well-being and survival. Let us not isolate the restrictions, reticences, evasions, or silences which all these procedures may have manifested, in order to refer them to some constitutive taboo, psychical repression, or death instinct. What was formed was a political ordering of life, not through an enslavement of others, but through an affirmation of self. And this was far from being a matter of the class which in the eighteenth century became hegemonic believing itself obliged to amputate from its body a sex that was useless, expensive, and dangerous as soon as it was no longer given over exclusively to reproduction; we can assert on the contrary that it provided itself with a body to be cared for, protected, cultivated, and preserved from the many dangers and contacts, to be isolated from others so that it would retain its differential value; and this, by equipping itself with —among other resources—a technology of sex.

Sex is not that part of the body which the bourgeoisie was forced to disqualify or nullify in order to put those whom it dominated to work. It is that aspect of itself which troubled and preoccupied it more than any other, begged and obtained its attention, and which it cultivated with a mixture of fear, curiosity, delight, and excitement. The bourgeoisie made this element identical with its body, or at least subordinated the latter to the former by attributing to it a mysterious and undefined power; it staked its life and its death on sex by making it responsible for its future welfare; it placed its hopes for the future in sex by imagining it to have ineluctable effects on generations to come; it subordinated its soul to sex by conceiving of it as what constituted the soul's most secret and determinant part. Let us not picture the bourgeoisie symbolically castrating itself the better to refuse others the right to have a sex and make use of it as they please. This class must be seen rather as being occupied, from the mid-eighteenth century on, with creating its own sexuality and forming a specific body based on it, a "class" body with its health, hygiene, descent, and race: the autosexualization of its body, the incarnation of sex in its body, the endogamy of sex and the body.

There were doubtless many reasons for this. First of all, there was a transposition into different forms of the methods employed by the nobility for marking and maintaining its caste distinction; for the aristocracy had also asserted the special character of its body, but this was in the form of *blood,* that is, in the form of the antiquity of its ancestry and of the value of its alliances; the bourgeoisie on the contrary looked to its progeny and the health of its organism when it laid claim to a specific body. The bourgeoisie's "blood" was its sex. And this is more than a play on words; many of the themes characteristic of the caste manners of the nobility reappeared in the nineteenth-century bourgeoisie, but in the guise of biological, medical, or eugenic precepts. The concern with genealogy became a preoccupation with heredity; but included in bourgeois marriages were not only economic imperatives and rules of social homogeneity, not only the promises of inheritance, but the menaces of heredity; families wore and concealed a sort of reversed and somber escutcheon whose defamatory quarters were the diseases or defects of the group of relatives—the grandfather's general paralysis, the mother's neurasthenia, the youngest child's phthisis, the hysterical or erotomanic aunts, the cousins with bad morals. But there was more to this concern with the sexual body than the bourgeois transposition of themes of the nobility for the purpose of self-affirmation. A different project was also involved: that of the indefinite extension of strength, vigor, health, and life. The emphasis on the body should undoubtedly be linked to the process of growth and establishment of bourgeois hegemony: not, however, because of the market value assumed by labor capacity, but because of what the "cultivation" of its own body could represent politically, economically, and historically for the present and the future of the bourgeoisie. Its dominance was in part dependent on that cultivation; but it was not simply a matter of economy or ideology, it was a "physical" matter as well. The works, published in great numbers at the end of the eighteenth century, on body hygiene, the art of longevity, ways of having healthy children and of keeping them alive as long as possible, and methods for improving the human lineage, bear witness to the fact: they thus attest to the correlation of this concern with the body and sex to a type of "racism." But the latter was very different from that manifested by the nobility and organized for basically conservative ends. It was a dynamic racism, a racism of expansion, even if it was still in a budding state, awaiting the second half of the nineteenth century to bear the fruits that we have tasted.

May I be forgiven by those for whom the bourgeoisie signifies the elision of the body and the repression of sexuality, for whom class struggle implies the fight to eliminate that repression; the "spontaneous philosophy" of the bourgeoisie is perhaps not as idealistic or castrating as is commonly thought. In any event, one of its primary concerns was to provide itself with a body and a sexuality—to ensure the strength, endurance, and secular proliferation of that body through the organization of a deployment of sexuality. This process, moreover, was linked to the movement by which it asserted its distinctiveness and its hegemony. There is little question that one of the primordial forms of class consciousness is the affirmation of the body; at least, this was the case for the bourgeoisie during the eighteenth century. It converted the blue blood of the nobles into a sound organism and a healthy sexuality. One understands why it took such a long time and was so unwilling to acknowledge that other classes had a body and a sex—precisely those classes it was exploiting. The living conditions that were dealt to the proletariat, particularly in the first half of the nineteenth century, show there was anything but concern for its body and sex:[1] it was of little importance whether *those* people lived or died, since their reproduction was something that took care of itself in any case. Conflicts were necessary (in particular, conflicts over urban space: cohabitation, proximity, contamination, epidemics, such as the cholera outbreak of 1832, or again, prostitution and venereal diseases) in order for the proletariat to be granted a body and a sexuality; economic emergencies had to arise (the development of heavy industry with the need for a stable and competent labor force, the obligation to regulate the population flow and apply demographic controls); lastly, there had to be established a whole technology of control which made it possible to keep that body and sexuality, finally conceded to them, under surveillance (schooling, the politics of housing, public hygiene, institutions of relief and insurance, the general medicalization of the population, in short, an entire administrative and technical machinery made it possible to safely import the deployment of sexuality into the exploited class; the latter no longer risked playing an assertive class role opposite the bourgeoisie; it would remain the instrument of the bourgeoisie's

[1] Cf. Karl Marx, "The Greed for Surplus-Labor," *Capital,* trans. Samuel Moore and Edward Aveling (New York: International Publishers, 1970), vol. 1, chap. 10, 2, pp. 235–43.

hegemony). Whence no doubt the proletariat's hesitancy to accept this deployment and its tendency to say that this sexuality was the business of the the bourgeoisie and did not concern it.

Some think they can denounce two symmetrical hypocrisies at the same time: the primary hypocrisy of the bourgeoisie which denies its own sexuality, and the secondary hypocrisy of the proletariat which in turn rejects its sexuality by accepting the dominant ideology. This is to misunderstand the process whereby on the contrary the bourgeoisie endowed itself, in an arrogant political affirmation, with a garrulous sexuality which the proletariat long refused to accept, since it was foisted on them for the purpose of subjugation. If it is true that sexuality is the set of effects produced in bodies, behaviors, and social relations by a certain deployment deriving from a complex political technology, one has to admit that this deployment does not operate in symmetrical fashion with respect to the social classes, and consequently, that it does not produce the same effects in them. We must return, therefore, to formulations that have long been disparaged; we must say that there is a bourgeois sexuality, and that there are class sexualities. Or rather, that sexuality is originally, historically bourgeois, and that, in its successive shifts and transpositions, it induces specific class effects.

A few more words are in order. As we have noted, the nineteenth century witnessed a generalization of the deployment of sexuality, starting from a hegemonic center. Eventually the entire social body was provided with a "sexual body," although this was accomplished in different ways and using different tools. Must we speak of the universality of sexuality, then? It is at this point that one notes the introduction of a new differentiating element. Somewhat similar to the way in which, at the end of the eighteenth century, the bourgeoisie set its own body and its precious sexuality against the valorous blood of the nobles, at the end of the nineteenth century it sought to redefine the specific character of its sexuality relative to that of others, subjecting it to a thorough differential review, and tracing a dividing line that would set apart and protect its body. This line was not the same as the one which founded sexuality, but rather a bar running through that sexuality; this was the taboo that constituted the difference, or at least the manner in which the taboo was applied and the rigor with which it was imposed. It was here that the theory of repression—which was gradually expanded to cover the entire deployment of sexuality, so that the latter came to be explained in terms of a generalized taboo—had its point of origin. This theory is bound up historically with the spread of the deployment of sexuality. On the one hand, the theory would justify its authoritarian and constraining influence by postulating that all sexuality must be subject to the law; more precisely, that sexuality owes its very definition to the action of the law: not only will you submit your sexuality to the law, but you will have no sexuality except by subjecting yourself to the law. But on the other hand, the theory of repression would compensate for this general spread of the deployment of sexuality by its analysis of the differential interplay of taboos according to the social classes. The discourse which at the end of the eighteenth century said: "There is a valuable element within us that must be feared and treated with respect; we must exercise extreme care in dealing with it, lest it be the cause of countless evils," was replaced by a discourse which said: "Our sexuality, unlike that of others, is subjected to a regime of repression so intense as to present a constant danger; not only is sex a formidable secret, as the directors of conscience, moralists, pedagogues, and doctors always said to former generations, not only must we search it out for the truth it conceals, but if it carries with it so many dangers, this is because—whether out of scrupulousness, an overly acute sense of sin, or hypocrisy, no matter—we have too long reduced it to silence." Henceforth social differentiation would be affirmed, not by the "sexual" quality of the body, but by the intensity of its repression.

Psychoanalysis comes in at this juncture: both a theory of the essential interrelatedness of the law and desire, and a technique for relieving the effects of the taboo where its rigor makes it pathogenic. In its historical emergence, psychoanalysis cannot be dissociated from the generalization of the deployment of sexuality and the secondary mechanisms of differentiation that resulted from it. The problem of incest is still significant in this regard. On one hand, as we have seen, its prohibition was posited as an absolutely universal principle which made it possible to explain both the system of alliance and the regime of sexuality; this taboo, in one form or another, was valid therefore for every society and every individual. But in practice psychoanalysis gave itself the task of alleviating the effects of repression (for those who were in a position to resort to psychoanalysis) that this prohibition was capable of causing; it allowed individuals to express their incestuous desire in discourse. But during the same period, there was a systematic campaign being organized against the kinds of incestuous practices that existed in rural areas or in certain urban quarters inaccessible to psychiatry: an intensive administrative and judicial grid was laid out then to put an end to these practices. An entire politics for the protection of children, or the placing of "endangered" minors under guardianship had as its partial objective their withdrawal from families that were suspected—through lack of space, dubious proximity, a history of debauchery, antisocial "primitiveness," or degenerescence—of practicing incest. Whereas the deployment of sexuality had been intensifying affective relations and physical proximity since the eighteenth century, and although there had occurred a perpetual incitement to incest in the bourgeois family, the regime of sexuality applied to the lower classes on the contrary involved the exclusion of incestuous practices or at least their displacement into another form. At a time when incest was being hunted out as a conduct, psychoanalysis was busy revealing it as a desire and alleviating—for those who suffered from the desire—the severity which repressed it. We must not forget that the discovery of the Oedipus complex was contemporaneous with the juridical organization of loss of parental authority (in France, this was formulated in the laws of 1889 and 1898). At the moment when Freud was uncovering the nature of Dora's desire and allowing it to be put into words, preparations were being made to undo those reprehensible proximities in other social sectors; on the one hand, the father was elevated into an object of compulsory love, but on the other hand, if he was a loved one, he was at the same time a fallen one in the eyes of the law. Psychoanalysis, as a limited therapeutic practice, thus played a differentiating role with respect to other procedures, within a deployment of sexuality that had come into general use. Those who had lost the exclusive privilege of worrying over their sexuality henceforth had the privilege of experiencing more than others the thing that prohibited it and of possessing the method which made it possible to remove the repression.

The history of the deployment of sexuality, as it has evolved since the classical age, can serve as an archaeology of psychoanalysis. We have seen in fact that psychoanalysis plays several roles at once in this deployment: it is a mechanism for attaching sexuality to the system of alliance; it assumes an adversary position with respect to the theory of degenerescence; it functions as a differentiating factor in the general technology of sex. Around it the great requirement of confession that had taken form so long ago assumed the new meaning of an injunction to lift psychical repression. The task of truth was now linked to the challenging of taboos.

This same development, moreover, opened up the possibility of a substantial shift in tactics, consisting in: reinterpreting the deployment of sexuality in terms of a generalized repression; tying this repression to general mechanisms of domination and exploitation; and linking together the processes that make it possible to free oneself both of repression and of domination and exploitation. Thus between the two world wars there was formed, around Reich, the historico-political critique of sexual repression. The importance of this critique and its impact on reality were substantial. But the very possibility of its success was tied to the fact that it always unfolded within the deployment of sexuality, and not outside or against it. The fact that so many things were able to change in the sexual behavior of Western societies without any of the promises or political conditions predicted by Reich being realized is sufficient proof that this whole sexual "revolution," this whole "antirepressive" struggle, represented nothing more, but nothing less—and its importance is undeniable—than a tactical shift and reversal in the great deployment of sexuality. But it is also apparent why one could not expect this critique to be the grid for a history of that very deployment. Nor the basis for a movement to dismantle it.

PART FIVE

*Right of Death
and Power over Life*

For a long time, one of the characteristic privileges of sovereign power was the right to decide life and death. In a formal sense, it derived no doubt from the ancient *patria potestas* that granted the father of the Roman family the right to "dispose" of the life of his children and his slaves; just as he had given them life, so he could take it away. By the time the right of life and death was framed by the classical theoreticians, it was in a considerably diminished form. It was no longer considered that this power of the sovereign over his subjects could be exercised in an absolute and unconditional way, but only in cases where the sovereign's very existence was in jeopardy: a sort of right of rejoinder. If he were threatened by external enemies who sought to overthrow him or contest his rights, he could then legitimately wage war, and require his subjects to take part in the defense of the state; without "directly proposing their death," he was empowered to "expose their life": in this sense, he wielded an "indirect" power over them of life and death.[1] But if someone dared to rise up against him and transgress his laws, then he could exercise a direct power over the offender's life: as punishment, the latter would be put to death. Viewed in this way, the power of life and death was not an absolute privilege: it was conditioned by the defense of the sovereign, and his own survival. Must we follow Hobbes in seeing it as the transfer to the prince of the natural right possessed by every individual to defend his life even if this meant the death of others? Or should it be regarded as a specific right that was manifested with the formation of that new juridical being,

[1] Samuel von Pufendorf, *Le Droit de la nature* (French trans., 1734), p. 445.

the sovereign?[2] In any case, in its modern form—relative and limited–as in its ancient and absolute form, the right of life and death is a dissymmetrical one. The sovereign exercised his right of life only by exercising his right to kill, or by refraining from killing; he evidenced his power over life only through the death he was capable of requiring. The right which was formulated as the "power of life and death" was in reality the right to *take* life or *let* live. Its symbol, after all, was the sword. Perhaps this juridical form must be referred to a historical type of society in which power was exercised mainly as a means of deduction *(prélèvement),* a subtraction mechanism, a right to appropriate a portion of the wealth, a tax of products, goods and services, labor and blood, levied on the subjects. Power in this instance was essentially a right of seizure: of things, time, bodies, and ultimately life itself; it culminated in the privilege to seize hold of life in order to suppress it.

Since the classical age the West has undergone a very profound transformation of these mechanisms of power. "Deduction" has tended to be no longer the major form of power but merely one element among others, working to incite, reinforce, control, monitor, optimize, and organize the forces under it: a power bent on generating forces, making them grow, and ordering them, rather than one dedicated to impeding them, making them submit, or destroying them. There has been a parallel shift in the right of death, or at least a tendency to align itself with the exigencies of a life-administering power and to define itself accordingly. This death that was based on the right of the sovereign is now manifested as simply the reverse of the right of the social body to ensure, maintain, or develop its life. Yet wars were never as bloody as they have been since the nineteenth century, and all things

[2] "Just as a composite body can have properties not found in any of the simple bodies of which the mixture consists, so a moral body, by virtue of the very union of persons of which it is composed, can have certain rights which none of the individuals could expressly claim and whose exercise is the proper function of leaders alone." Pufendorf, *Le Droit de la nature,* p. 452.

being equal, never before did regimes visit such holocausts on their own populations. But this formidable power of death —and this is perhaps what accounts for part of its force and the cynicism with which it has so greatly expanded its limits —now presents itself as the counterpart of a power that exerts a positive influence on life, that endeavors to administer, optimize, and multiply it, subjecting it to precise controls and comprehensive regulations. Wars are no longer waged in the name of a sovereign who must be defended; they are waged on behalf of the existence of everyone; entire populations are mobilized for the purpose of wholesale slaughter in the name of life necessity: massacres have become vital. It is as managers of life and survival, of bodies and the race, that so many regimes have been able to wage so many wars, causing so many men to be killed. And through a turn that closes the circle, as the technology of wars has caused them to tend increasingly toward all-out destruction, the decision that initiates them and the one that terminates them are in fact increasingly informed by the naked question of survival. The atomic situation is now at the end point of this process: the power to expose a whole population to death is the underside of the power to guarantee an individual's continued existence. The principle underlying the tactics of battle—that one has to be capable of killing in order to go on living—has become the principle that defines the strategy of states. But the existence in question is no longer the juridical existence of sovereignty; at stake is the biological existence of a population. If genocide is indeed the dream of modern powers, this is not because of a recent return of the ancient right to kill; it is because power is situated and exercised at the level of life, the species, the race, and the large-scale phenomena of population.

On another level, I might have taken up the example of the death penalty. Together with war, it was for a long time the other form of the right of the sword; it constituted the reply of the sovereign to those who attacked his will, his law, or his person. Those who died on the scaffold became fewer and fewer, in contrast to those who died in wars. But it was for the same reasons that the latter became more numerous and the former more and more rare. As soon as power gave itself the function of administering life, its reason for being and the logic of its exercise—and not the awakening of humanitarian feelings—made it more and more difficult to apply the death penalty. How could power exercise its highest prerogatives by putting people to death, when its main role was to ensure, sustain, and multiply life, to put this life in order? For such a power, execution was at the same time a limit, a scandal, and a contradiction. Hence capital punishment could not be maintained except by invoking less the enormity of the crime itself than the monstrosity of the criminal, his incorrigibility, and the safeguard of society. One had the right to kill those who represented a kind of biological danger to others.

One might say that the ancient right to *take* life or *let* live was replaced by a power to *foster* life or *disallow* it to the point of death. This is perhaps what explains that disqualification of death which marks the recent wane of the rituals that accompanied it. That death is so carefully evaded is linked less to a new anxiety which makes death unbearable for our societies than to the fact that the procedures of power have not ceased to turn away from death. In the passage from this world to the other, death was the manner in which a terrestrial sovereignty was relieved by another, singularly more powerful sovereignty; the pageantry that surrounded it was in the category of political ceremony. Now it is over life, throughout its unfolding, that power establishes its dominion; death is power's limit, the moment that escapes it; death becomes the most secret aspect of existence, the most "private." It is not surprising that suicide—once a crime, since it was a way to usurp the power of death which the sovereign alone, whether the one here below or the Lord above, had the right to exercise—became, in the course of the nineteenth century, one of the first conducts to enter into the sphere of sociological analysis; it testified to the individual and private right to die, at the borders and in the interstices of power that was exercised over life. This determination to die, strange and yet so persistent and constant in its manifestations, and consequently so difficult to explain as being due to particular circumstances or individual accidents, was one of the first astonishments of a society in which political power had assigned itself the task of administering life.

In concrete terms, starting in the seventeenth century, this power over life evolved in two basic forms; these forms were not antithetical, however; they constituted rather two poles of development linked together by a whole intermediary cluster of relations. One of these poles—the first to be formed, it seems—centered on the body as a machine: its disciplining, the optimization of its capabilities, the extortion of its forces, the parallel increase of its usefulness and its docility, its integration into systems of efficient and economic controls, all this was ensured by the procedures of power that characterized the *disciplines: an anatomo-politics of the human body.* The second, formed somewhat later, focused on the species body, the body imbued with the mechanics of life and serving as the basis of the biological processes: propagation, births and mortality, the level of health, life expectancy and longevity, with all the conditions that can cause these to vary. Their supervision was effected through an entire series of interventions and *regulatory controls: a biopolitics of the population.* The disciplines of the body and the regulations of the population constituted the two poles around which the organization of power over life was deployed. The setting up, in the course of the classical age, of this great bipolar technology—anatomic and biological, individualizing and specifying, directed toward the performances of the body, with attention to the processes of life—characterized a power whose highest function was perhaps no longer to kill, but to invest life through and through.

The old power of death that symbolized sovereign power

was now carefully supplanted by the administration of bodies and the calculated management of life. During the classical period, there was a rapid development of various disciplines —universities, secondary schools, barracks, workshops; there was also the emergence, in the field of political practices and economic observation, of the problems of birthrate, longevity, public health, housing, and migration. Hence there was an explosion of numerous and diverse techniques for achieving the subjugation of bodies and the control of populations, marking the beginning of an era of "bio-power." The two directions taken by its development still appeared to be clearly separate in the eighteenth century. With regard to discipline, this development was embodied in institutions such as the army and the schools, and in reflections on tactics, apprenticeship, education, and the nature of societies, ranging from the strictly military analyses of Marshal de Saxe to the political reveries of Guibert or Servan. As for population controls, one notes the emergence of demography, the evaluation of the relationship between resources and inhabitants, the constructing of tables analyzing wealth and its circulation: the work of Quesnay, Moheau, and Süssmilch. The philosophy of the "Ideologists," as a theory of ideas, signs, and the individual genesis of sensations, but also a theory of the social composition of interests—Ideology being a doctrine of apprenticeship, but also a doctrine of contracts and the regulated formation of the social body— no doubt constituted the abstract discourse in which one sought to coordinate these two techniques of power in order to construct a general theory of it. In point of fact, however, they were not to be joined at the level of a speculative discourse, but in the form of concrete arrangements *(agencements concrets)* that would go to make up the great technology of power in the nineteenth century: the deployment of sexuality would be one of them, and one of the most important.

This bio-power was without question an indispensable element in the development of capitalism; the latter would not have been possible without the controlled insertion of bodies into the machinery of production and the adjustment of the phenomena of population to economic processes. But this was not all it required; it also needed the growth of both these factors, their reinforcement as well as their availability and docility; it had to have methods of power capable of optimizing forces, aptitudes, and life in general without at the same time making them more difficult to govern. If the development of the great instruments of the state, as *institutions* of power, ensured the maintenance of production relations, the rudiments of anatomo- and bio-politics, created in the eighteenth century as *techniques* of power present at every level of the social body and utilized by very diverse institutions (the family and the army, schools and the police, individual medicine and the administration of collective bodies), operated in the sphere of economic processes, their development, and the forces working to sustain them. They also acted as factors of segregation and social hierarchization, exerting their influence on the respective forces of both these movements, guaranteeing relations of domination and effects of hegemony. The adjustment of the accumulation of men to that of capital, the joining of the growth of human groups to the expansion of productive forces and the differential allocation of profit, were made possible in part by the exercise of bio-power in its many forms and modes of application. The investment of the body, its valorization, and the distributive management of its forces were at the time indispensable.

One knows how many times the question has been raised concerning the role of an ascetic morality in the first formation of capitalism; but what occurred in the eighteenth century in some Western countries, an event bound up with the development of capitalism, was a different phenomenon having perhaps a wider impact than the new morality; this was nothing less than the entry of life into history, that is, the entry of phenomena peculiar to the life of the human species into the order of knowledge and power, into the sphere of political techniques. It is not a question of claiming that this was the moment when the first contact between life and history was brought about. On the contrary, the pressure exerted by the biological on the historical had remained very strong for thousands of years; epidemics and famine were the two great dramatic forms of this relationship that was always dominated by the menace of death. But through a circular process, the economic—and primarily agricultural—development of the eighteenth century, and an increase in productivity and resources even more rapid than the demographic growth it encouraged, allowed a measure of relief from these profound threats: despite some renewed outbreaks, the period of great ravages from starvation and plague had come to a close before the French Revolution; death was ceasing to torment life so directly. But at the same time, the development of the different fields of knowledge concerned with life in general, the improvement of agricultural techniques, and the observations and measures relative to man's life and survival contributed to this relaxation: a relative control over life averted some of the imminent risks of death. In the space for movement thus conquered, and broadening and organizing that space, methods of power and knowledge assumed responsibility for the life processes and undertook to control and modify them. Western man was gradually learning what it meant to be a living species in a living world, to have a body, conditions of existence, probabilities of life, an individual and collective welfare, forces that could be modified, and a space in which they could be distributed in an optimal manner. For the first time in history, no doubt, biological existence was reflected in political existence; the fact of living was no longer an inaccessible substrate that only emerged from time to time, amid the randomness of death and its fatality; part of it passed into knowledge's field of control and power's sphere of intervention. Power would no longer be dealing simply with legal subjects over whom the ultimate dominion was death, but with living beings, and the mastery it would be able to exercise over them would have to be applied at the level of life itself; it was the taking charge of life, more than the threat of death, that gave power its access even to the body. If one can apply the term *bio-history* to the pressures through which the movements of life and the processes of history interfere with one another, one would have to speak of *bio-power* to designate what brought life and its mechanisms into the realm of explicit calculations and made knowledge-power an agent of transformation of human life. It is not that life has been totally integrated into techniques that govern and administer it; it constantly escapes them. Outside the Western world, famine exists, on a greater scale than ever; and the biological risks confronting the species are perhaps greater, and certainly more serious, than before the birth of microbiology. But what might be called a society's "threshold of modernity" has been reached when the life of the species is wagered on its own political strategies. For millennia, man remained what he was for Aristotle: a living animal with the additional capacity for a political existence; modern man is an animal whose politics places his existence as a living being in question.

This transformation had considerable consequences. It would serve no purpose here to dwell on the rupture that occurred then in the pattern of scientific discourse and on the manner in which the twofold problematic of life and man disrupted and redistributed the order of the classical episteme. If the question of man was raised—insofar as he was a specific living being, and specifically related to other living beings—the reason for this is to be sought in the new mode of relation between history and life: in this dual position of life that placed it at the same time outside history, in its biological environment, and inside human historicity, penetrated by the latter's techniques of knowledge and power. There is no need either to lay further stress on the proliferation of political technologies that ensued, investing the body, health, modes of subsistence and habitation, living conditions, the whole space of existence.

Another consequence of this development of bio-power was the growing importance assumed by the action of the norm, at the expense of the juridical system of the law. Law cannot help but but be armed, and its arm, *par excellence,* is death; to those who transgress it, it replies, at least as a last resort, with that absolute menace. The law always refers to the sword. But a power whose task is to take charge of life needs continuous regulatory and corrective mechanisms. It is no longer a matter of bringing death into play in the field of sovereignty, but of distributing the living in the domain of value and utility. Such a power has to qualify, measure, appraise, and hierarchize, rather than display itself in its murderous splendor; it does not have to draw the line that separates the enemies of the sovereign from his obedient subjects; it effects distributions around the norm. I do not mean to say that the law fades into the background or that the institutions of justice tend to disappear, but rather that the law operates more and more as a norm, and that the judicial institution is increasingly incorporated into a continuum of apparatuses (medical, administrative, and so on) whose functions are for the most part regulatory. A normalizing society is the historical outcome of a technology of power centered on life. We have entered a phase of juridical regression in comparison with the pre-seventeenth-century societies we are acquainted with; we should not be deceived by all the Constitutions framed throughout the world since the French Revolution, the Codes written and revised, a whole continual and clamorous legislative activity: these were the forms that made an essentially normalizing power acceptable.

Moreover, against this power that was still new in the nineteenth century, the forces that resisted relied for support on the very thing it invested, that is, on life and man as a living being. Since the last century, the great struggles that

have challenged the general system of power were not guided
by the belief in a return to former rights, or by the age-old
dream of a cycle of time or a Golden Age. One no longer
aspired toward the coming of the emperor of the poor, or the
kingdom of the latter days, or even the restoration of our
imagined ancestral rights; what was demanded and what
served as an objective was life, understood as the basic needs,
man's concrete essence, the realization of his potential, a
plenitude of the possible. Whether or not it was Utopia that
was wanted is of little importance; what we have seen has
been a very real process of struggle; life as a political object
was in a sense taken at face value and turned back against
the system that was bent on controlling it. It was life more
than the law that became the issue of political struggles, even
if the latter were formulated through affirmations concerning
rights. The "right" to life, to one's body, to health, to happiness, to the satisfaction of needs, and beyond all the oppres-
sions or "alienations," the "right" to rediscover what one is
and all that one can be, this "right"—which the classical
juridical system was utterly incapable of comprehending—
was the political response to all these new procedures of
power which did not derive, either, from the traditional right
of sovereignty.

This is the background that enables us to understand the
importance assumed by sex as a political issue. It was at the
pivot of the two axes along which developed the entire political technology of life. On the one hand it was tied to the
disciplines of the body: the harnessing, intensification, and
distribution of forces, the adjustment and economy of energies. On the other hand, it was applied to the regulation of
populations, through all the far-reaching effects of its activity. It fitted in both categories at once, giving rise to infinitesimal surveillances, permanent controls, extremely meticulous
orderings of space, indeterminate medical or psychological
examinations, to an entire micro-power concerned with the

body. But it gave rise as well to comprehensive measures, statistical assessments, and interventions aimed at the entire social body or at groups taken as a whole. Sex was a means of access both to the life of the body and the life of the species. It was employed as a standard for the disciplines and as a basis for regulations. This is why in the nineteenth century sexuality was sought out in the smallest details of individual existences; it was tracked down in behavior, pursued in dreams; it was suspected of underlying the least follies, it was traced back into the earliest years of childhood; it became the stamp of individuality—at the same time what enabled one to analyze the latter and what made it possible to master it. But one also sees it becoming the theme of political operations, economic interventions (through incitements to or curbs on procreation), and ideological campaigns for raising standards of morality and responsibility: it was put forward as the index of a society's strength, revealing of both its political energy and its biological vigor. Spread out from one pole to the other of this technology of sex was a whole series of different tactics that combined in varying proportions the objective of disciplining the body and that of regulating populations.

Whence the importance of the four great lines of attack along which the politics of sex advanced for two centuries. Each one was a way of combining disciplinary techniques with regulative methods. The first two rested on the requirements of regulation, on a whole thematic of the species, descent, and collective welfare, in order to obtain results at the level of discipline; the sexualization of children was accomplished in the form of a campaign for the health of the race (precocious sexuality was presented from the eighteenth century to the end of the nineteenth as an epidemic menace that risked compromising not only the future health of adults but the future of the entire society and species); the hysterization of women, which involved a thorough medicalization of their bodies and their sex, was carried out in the name of the responsibility they owed to the health of their children, the solidity of the family institution, and the safeguarding of society. It was the reverse relationship that applied in the case of birth controls and the psychiatrization of perversions: here the intervention was regulatory in nature, but it had to rely on the demand for individual disciplines and constraints *(dressages).* Broadly speaking, at the juncture of the "body" and the "population," sex became a crucial target of a power organized around the management of life rather than the menace of death.

The blood relation long remained an important element in the mechanisms of power, its manifestations, and its rituals. For a society in which the systems of alliance, the political form of the sovereign, the differentiation into orders and castes, and the value of descent lines were predominant; for a society in which famine, epidemics, and violence made death imminent, blood constituted one of the fundamental values. It owed its high value at the same time to its instrumental role (the ability to shed blood), to the way it functioned in the order of signs (to have a certain blood, to be of the same blood, to be prepared to risk one's blood), and also to its precariousness (easily spilled, subject to drying up, too readily mixed, capable of being quickly corrupted). A society of blood—I was tempted to say, of "sanguinity"—where power spoke *through* blood: the honor of war, the fear of famine, the triumph of death, the sovereign with his sword, executioners, and tortures; blood was *a reality with a symbolic function.* We, on the other hand, are in a society of "sex," or rather a society "with a sexuality": the mechanisms of power are addressed to the body, to life, to what causes it to proliferate, to what reinforces the species, its stamina, its ability to dominate, or its capacity for being used. Through the themes of health, progeny, race, the future of the species, the vitality of the social body, power spoke *of* sexuality and *to* sexuality; the latter was not a mark or a symbol, it was an object and a target. Moreover, its importance was due less to its rarity or its precariousness than to its insistence, its insidious presence, the fact that it was everywhere an object of excitement and fear at the same time. Power delineated it, aroused it, and employed it as the proliferating meaning that had always to be taken control of again lest it escape; it was *an effect with a meaning-value.* I do not mean to say that a substitution of sex for blood was by itself responsible for all the transformations that marked the threshold of our modernity. It is not the soul of two civilizations or the organizing principle of two cultural forms that I am attempting to express; I am looking for the reasons for which sexuality, far from being repressed in the society of that period, on the contrary was constantly aroused. The new procedures of power that were devised during the classical age and employed in the nineteenth century were what caused our societies to go from *a symbolics of blood* to *an analytics of sexuality.* Clearly, nothing was more on the side of the law, death, transgression, the symbolic, and sovereignty than blood; just as sexuality was on the side of the norm, knowledge, life, meaning, the disciplines, and regulations.

Sade and the first eugenists were contemporary with this transition from "sanguinity" to "sexuality." But whereas the first dreams of the perfecting of the species inclined the whole problem toward an extremely exacting administration of sex (the art of determining good marriages, of inducing the desired fertilities, of ensuring the health and longevity of children), and while the new concept of race tended to obliterate the aristocratic particularities of blood, retaining only the controllable effects of sex, Sade carried the exhaustive analysis of sex over into the mechanisms of the old power of sovereignty and endowed it with the ancient but fully maintained prestige of blood; the latter flowed through the whole dimension of pleasure—the blood of torture and absolute power, the blood of the caste which was respected in itself and which nonetheless was made to flow in the major rituals of parricide and incest, the blood of the people, which was shed unreservedly since the sort that flowed in its veins was not even deserving of a name. In Sade, sex is without any norm or intrinsic rule that might be formulated from its own nature; but it is subject to the unrestricted law of a power which itself knows no other law but its own; if by chance it is at times forced to accept the order of progressions carefully disciplined into successive days, this exercise carries it to a point where it is no longer anything but a unique and naked sovereignty: an unlimited right of all-powerful monstrosity.

While it is true that the analytics of sexuality and the symbolics of blood were grounded at first in two very distinct regimes of power, in actual fact the passage from one to the other did not come about (any more than did these powers themselves) without overlappings, interactions, and echoes. In different ways, the preoccupation with blood and the law has for nearly two centuries haunted the administration of sexuality. Two of these interferences are noteworthy, the one for its historical importance, the other for the problems it poses. Beginning in the second half of the nineteenth century, the thematics of blood was sometimes called on to lend its entire historical weight toward revitalizing the type of political power that was exercised through the devices of sexuality. Racism took shape at this point (racism in its modern, "biologizing," statist form): it was then that a whole politics of settlement *(peuplement),* family, marriage, education, social hierarchization, and property, accompanied by a long series of permanent interventions at the level of the body, conduct, health, and everyday life, received their color and their justification from the mythical concern with protecting the purity of the blood and ensuring the triumph of the race. Nazism was doubtless the most cunning and the most naïve (and the former because of the latter) combination of the fantasies of blood and the paroxysms of a disciplinary power. A eugenic ordering of society, with all that implied in the way of extension and intensification of micro-powers, in the guise of an unrestricted state control *(étatisation),* was accompanied by the oneiric exaltation of a superior blood; the latter implied both the systematic genocide of others and the risk of exposing oneself to a total sacrifice. It is an irony of history that the Hitlerite politics of sex remained an insignificant practice while the blood myth was transformed into the greatest blood bath in recent memory.

At the opposite extreme, starting from this same end of the nineteenth century, we can trace the theoretical effort to reinscribe the thematic of sexuality in the system of law, the symbolic order, and sovereignty. It is to the political credit of psychoanalysis—or at least, of what was most coherent in it—that it regarded with suspicion (and this from its inception, that is, from the moment it broke away from the neuropsychiatry of degenerescence) the irrevocably proliferating aspects which might be contained in these power mechanisms aimed at controlling and administering the everyday life of sexuality: whence the Freudian endeavor (out of reaction no doubt to the great surge of racism that was contemporary with it) to ground sexuality in the law—the law of alliance, tabooed consanguinity, and the Sovereign-Father, in short, to surround desire with all the trappings of the old order of power. It was owing to this that psychoanalysis was —in the main, with a few exceptions—in theoretical and practical opposition to fascism. But this position of psychoanalysis was tied to a specific historical conjuncture. And yet, to conceive the category of the sexual in terms of the law, death, blood, and sovereignty—whatever the references to Sade and Bataille, and however one might gauge their "subversive" influence—is in the last analysis a historical "retro-version." We must conceptualize the deployment of sexuality on the basis of the techniques of power that are contemporary with it.

People are going to say that I am dealing in a historicism which is more careless than radical; that I am evading the biologically established existence of sexual functions for the benefit of phenomena that are variable, perhaps, but fragile, secondary, and ultimately superficial; and that I speak of sexuality as if sex did not exist. And one would be entitled to object as follows: "You claim to analyze in detail the processes by which women's bodies, the lives of children, family relationships, and an entire network of social relations were sexualized. You wish to describe that great awakening of sexual concern since the eighteenth century and our growing eagerness to suspect the presence of sex in everything. Let us admit as much and suppose that the mechanisms of power were in fact used more to arouse and 'excite' sexuality than to repress it. But here you remain quite near to the thing you no doubt believe you have gotten away from; at bottom, when you point out phenomena of diffusion, anchorage, and fixation of sexuality, you are trying to reveal what might be called the organization of 'erotic zones' in the social body; it may well be the case that you have done nothing more than transpose to the level of diffuse processes mechanisms which psychoanalysis has identified with precision at the level of the individual. But you pass over the thing on the basis of which this sexualization was able to develop and which psychoanalysis does not fail to recognize—namely, sex. Before Freud, one sought to localize sexuality as closely as possible: in sex, in its reproductive functions, in its immediate anatomical localizations; one fell back upon a biological minimum: organ, instinct, and finality. You, on the other hand, are in a symmetrical and inverse position: for you, there remain only groundless effects, ramifications without roots, a sexuality without a sex. What is this if not castration once again?"

Here we need to distinguish between two questions. First, does the analysis of sexuality necessarily imply the elision of the body, anatomy, the biological, the functional? To this question, I think we can reply in the negative. In any case, the purpose of the present study is in fact to show how deployments of power are directly connected to the body—

to bodies, functions, physiological processes, sensations, and pleasures; far from the body having to be effaced, what is needed is to make it visible through an analysis in which the biological and the historical are not consecutive to one another, as in the evolutionism of the first sociologists, but are bound together in an increasingly complex fashion in accordance with the development of the modern technologies of power that take life as their objective. Hence I do not envisage a "history of mentalities" that would take account of bodies only through the manner in which they have been perceived and given meaning and value; but a "history of bodies" and the manner in which what is most material and most vital in them has been invested.

Another question, distinct from the first one: this materiality that is referred to, is it not, then, that of sex, and is it not paradoxical to venture a history of sexuality at the level of bodies, without there being the least question of sex? After all, is the power that is exercised through sexuality not directed specifically at that element of reality which is "sex," sex in general? That sexuality is not, in relation to power, an exterior domain to which power is applied, that on the contrary it is a result and an instrument of power's designs, is all very well. But as for sex, is it not the "other" with respect to power, while being the center around which sexuality distributes its effects? Now, it is precisely this idea of sex *in itself* that we cannot accept without examination. Is "sex" really the anchorage point that supports the manifestations of sexuality, or is it not rather a complex idea that was formed inside the deployment of sexuality? In any case, one could show how this idea of sex took form in the different strategies of power and the definite role it played therein.

All along the great lines which the development of the deployment of sexuality has followed since the nineteenth century, one sees the elaboration of this idea that there exists something other than bodies, organs, somatic localizations, functions, anatomo-physiological systems, sensations, and pleasures; something else and something more, with intrinsic properties and laws of its own: "sex." Thus, in the process of hysterization of women, "sex" was defined in three ways: as that which belongs in common to men and women; as that which belongs, *par excellence,* to men, and hence is lacking in women; but at the same time, as that which by itself constitutes woman's body, ordering it wholly in terms of the functions of reproduction and keeping it in constant agitation through the effects of that very function. Hysteria was interpreted in this strategy as the movement of sex insofar as it was the "one" and the "other," whole and part, principle and lack. In the sexualization of childhood, there was formed the idea of a sex that was both present (from the evidence of anatomy) and absent (from the standpoint of physiology), present too if one considered its activity, and deficient if one referred to its reproductive finality; or again, actual in its manifestations, but hidden in its eventual effects, whose pathological seriousness would only become apparent later. If the sex of the child was still present in the adult, it was in the form of a secret causality that tended to nullify the sex of the latter (it was one of the tenets of eighteenth- and nineteenth-century medicine that precocious sex would eventually result in sterility, impotence, frigidity, the inability to experience pleasure, or the deadening of the senses); by sexualizing childhood, the idea was established of a sex characterized essentially by the interplay of presence and absence, the visible and the hidden; masturbation and the effects imputed to it were thought to reveal in a privileged way this interplay of presence and absence, of the visible and the hidden.

In the psychiatrization of perversions, sex was related to biological functions and to an anatomo-physiological machinery that gave it its "meaning," that is, its finality; but it was also referred to an instinct which, through its peculiar development and according to the objects to which it could become attached, made it possible for perverse behavior patterns to arise and made their genesis intelligible. Thus "sex" was defined by the interlacing of function and instinct, finality and signification; moreover, this was the form in which it was manifested, more clearly than anywhere else, in the model perversion, in that "fetishism" which, from at least as early as 1877, served as the guiding thread for analyzing all the other deviations. In it one could clearly perceive the way in which the instinct became fastened to an object in accordance with an individual's historical adherence and biological inadequacy. Lastly, in the socialization of procreative behavior, "sex" was described as being caught between a law of reality (economic necessity being its most abrupt and immediate form) and an economy of pleasure which was always attempting to circumvent that law—when, that is, it did not ignore it altogether. The most notorious of "frauds," coitus interruptus, represented the point where the insistence of the real forced an end to pleasure and where the pleasure found a way to surface despite the economy dictated by the real. It is apparent that the deployment of sexuality, with its different strategies, was what established this notion of "sex"; and in the four major forms of hysteria, onanism, fetishism, and interrupted coition, it showed this sex to be governed by the interplay of whole and part, principle and lack, absence and presence, excess and deficiency, by the function of instinct, finality, and meaning, of reality and pleasure.

The theory thus generated performed a certain number of functions that made it indispensable. First, the notion of "sex" made it possible to group together, in an artificial unity, anatomical elements, biological functions, conducts, sensations, and pleasures, and it enabled one to make use of this fictitious unity as a causal principle, an omnipresent meaning, a secret to be discovered everywhere: sex was thus able to function as a unique signifier and as a universal signified. Further, by presenting itself in a unitary fashion, as anatomy and lack, as function and latency, as instinct and meaning, it was able to mark the line of contact between a knowledge of human sexuality and the biological sciences of reproduction; thus, without really borrowing anything from the these sciences, excepting a few doubtful analogies, the knowledge of sexuality gained through proximity a guarantee of quasi-scientificity; but by virtue of this same proximity, some of the contents of biology and physiology were able to serve as a principle of normality for human sexuality. Finally, the notion of sex brought about a fundamental reversal; it made it possible to invert the representation of the relationships of power to sexuality, causing the latter to appear, not in its essential and positive relation to power, but as being rooted in a specific and irreducible urgency which power tries as best it can to dominate; thus the idea of "sex" makes it possible to evade what gives "power" its power; it enables one to conceive power solely as law and taboo. Sex —that agency which appears to dominate us and that secret which seems to underlie all that we are, that point which enthralls us through the the power it manifests and the meaning it conceals, and which we ask to reveal what we are and to free us from what defines us—is doubtless but an ideal point made necessary by the deployment of sexuality and its operation. We must not make the mistake of thinking that sex is an autonomous agency which secondarily produces manifold effects of sexuality over the entire length of its surface of contact with power. On the contrary, sex is the most speculative, most ideal, and most internal element in a deployment of sexuality organized by power in its grip on bodies and their materiality, their forces, energies, sensations, and pleasures.

It might be added that "sex" performs yet another function that runs through and sustains the ones we have just examined. Its role in this instance is more practical than theoretical. It is through sex—in fact, an imaginary point determined by the deployment of sexuality—that each individual has to pass in order to have access to his own intelligibility (seeing that it is both the hidden aspect and the generative principle of meaning), to the whole of his body (since it is a real and threatened part of it, while symbolically constituting the whole), to his identity (since it joins the force of a drive to the singularity of a history). Through a reversal that doubtless had its surreptitious beginnings long ago—it was already making itself felt at the time of the Christian pastoral of the flesh—we have arrived at the point where we expect our intelligibility to come from what was for many centuries thought of as madness; the plenitude of our body from what was long considered its stigma and likened to a wound; our identity from what was perceived as an obscure and nameless urge. Hence the importance we ascribe to it, the reverential fear with which we surround it, the care we take to know it. Hence the fact that over the centuries it has become more important than our soul, more important almost than our life; and so it is that all the world's enigmas appear frivolous to us compared to this secret, minuscule in each of us, but of a density that makes it more serious than any other. The Faustian pact, whose temptation has been instilled in us by the deployment of sexuality, is now as follows: to exchange life in its entirety for sex itself, for the truth and the sovereignty of sex. Sex is worth dying for. It is in this (strictly historical) sense that sex is indeed imbued with the death instinct. When a long while ago the West discovered love, it bestowed on it a value high enough to make death acceptable; nowadays it is sex that claims this equivalence, the highest of all. And while the deployment of sexuality permits the techniques of power to invest life, the fictitious point of sex, itself marked by that deployment, exerts enough charm on everyone for them to accept hearing the grumble of death within it.

By creating the imaginary element that is "sex," the deployment of sexuality established one of its most essential internal operating principles: the desire for sex—the desire to have it, to have access to it, to discover it, to liberate it, to articulate it in discourse, to formulate it in truth. It constituted "sex" itself as something desirable. And it is this desirability of sex that attaches each one of us to the injunction to know it, to reveal its law and its power; it is this desirability that makes us think we are affirming the rights of our sex against all power, when in fact we are fastened to the deployment of sexuality that has lifted up from deep within us a sort of mirage in which we think we see ourselves reflected—the dark shimmer of sex.

"It is sex," said Kate in *The Plumed Serpent*. "How wonderful sex can be, when men keep it powerful and sacred, and it fills the world! like sunshine through and through one!"

So we must not refer a history of sexuality to the agency of sex; but rather show how "sex" is historically subordinate to sexuality. We must not place sex on the side of reality, and sexuality on that of confused ideas and illusions; sexuality is a very real historical formation; it is what gave rise to the notion of sex, as a speculative element necessary to its operation. We must not think that by saying yes to sex, one says no to power; on the contrary, one tracks along the course laid out by the general deployment of sexuality. It is the agency of sex that we must break away from, if we aim—through a tactical reversal of the various mechanisms of sexuality—to counter the grips of power with the claims of bodies, pleasures, and knowledges, in their multiplicity and their possibility of resistance. The rallying point for the counterattack against the deployment of sexuality ought not to be sex-desire, but bodies and pleasures.

"There has been so much action in the past," said D. H. Lawrence, "especially sexual action, a wearying repetition over and over, without a corresponding thought, a corresponding realization. Now our business is to realize sex. Today the full conscious realization of sex is even more important than the act itself."

Perhaps one day people will wonder at this. They will not be able to understand how a civilization so intent on developing enormous instruments of production and destruction found the time and the infinite patience to inquire so anxiously concerning the actual state of sex; people will smile perhaps when they recall that here were men—meaning ourselves—who believed that therein resided a truth every bit as precious as the one they had already demanded from the earth, the stars, and the pure forms of their thought; people will be surprised at the eagerness with which we went about pretending to rouse from its slumber a sexuality which everything—our discourses, our customs, our institutions, our regulations, our knowledges—was busy producing in the light of day and broadcasting to noisy accompaniment. And people will ask themselves why we were so bent on ending the rule of silence regarding what was the noisiest of our preoccupations. In retrospect, this noise may appear to have been out of place, but how much stranger will seem our persistence in interpreting it as but the refusal to speak and the order to remain silent. People will wonder what could have made us so presumptuous; they will look for the reasons that might explain why we prided ourselves on being the first to grant sex the importance we say is its due and how we came to congratulate ourselves for finally—in the twentieth century—having broken free of a long period of harsh repression, a protracted Christian asceticism, greedily and fastidiously adapted to the imperatives of bourgeois economy. And what we now perceive as the chronicle of a censorship and the difficult struggle to remove it will be seen rather as the centuries-long rise of a complex deployment for compelling sex to speak, for fastening our attention and concern upon sex, for getting us to believe in the sovereignty of its law when in fact we were moved by the power mechanisms of sexuality.

People will be amused at the reproach of pansexualism that was once aimed at Freud and psychoanalysis. But the ones who will appear to have been blind will perhaps be not so much those who formulated the objection as those who discounted it out of hand, as if it merely expressed the fears of an outmoded prudishness. For the first, after all, were only taken unawares by a process which had begun long before and by which, unbeknown to them, they were already surrounded on all sides; what they had attributed solely to the genius of Freud had already gone through a long stage of preparation; they had gotten their dates wrong as to the establishment, in our society, of a general deployment of sexuality. But the others were mistaken concerning the nature of the process; they believed that Freud had at last, through a sudden reversal, restored to sex the rightful share which it had been denied for so long; they had not seen how the good genius of Freud had placed it at one of the critical points marked out for it since the eighteenth century by the strategies of knowledge and power, how wonderfully effective he was—worthy of the greatest spiritual fathers and directors of the classical period—in giving a new impetus to the secular injunction to study sex and transform it into discourse. We are often reminded of the countless procedures which Christianity once employed to make us detest the body; but let us ponder all the ruses that were employed for centuries to make us love sex, to make the knowledge of it desirable and everything said about it precious. Let us consider the stratagems by which we were induced to apply all our skills to discovering its secrets, by which we were attached to the obligation to draw out its truth, and made guilty for having failed to recognize it for so long. These devices are what ought to make us wonder today. Moreover, we need to consider the possibility that one day, perhaps, in a different economy of bodies and pleasures, people will no longer quite understand how the ruses of sexuality, and the power that sustains its organization, were able to subject us to that austere monarchy of sex, so that we became dedicated to the endless task of forcing its secret, of exacting the truest of confessions from a shadow.

The irony of this deployment is in having us believe that our "liberation" is in the balance.

Index

sexual discourse, 17–35
  and censorship, 17–18, 21, 84
  about children's sex, 27–30
  in the confessional, 18–21, 35, 61–3. *See also* confession
  illicit, 4, 18
  on incest, 129–30
  in literature, 21–3, 59–60
  new sources in eighteenth and nineteenth centuries, 30–1
  pervasiveness of, 32–4
  and pleasure, 71
  political incitement to, 17–18, 34–5
  and power relationships, 97–8
  process of scientization, 53–73
  and the public interest, 23–6
  sanctions against perversion, 36–7
  and sodomy, 101
  valorization and enlargement of boundaries, 23
sexual initiation
  and *ars erotica,* 57
  compared to discourse, 62
sexual pleasure
  and *ars erotica,* 58
  confessional archives, 63–4
  perverse, 105
  See also pleasure
sexual practices
  and *ars erotica,* 57
  seventeenth-century frankness, 3
  three major codes regulating, 37–8
sexual repression
  advent of, 5, 17
  and class structure, 120–2
  denial of, 81–2
  distinguished from legal prohibition, 4
  economic and political motives, 5–6, 25–6
  in eighteenth-century schools, 27–30
  vs. expansion of sexual discourse, 17–18, 34–5, 72–3
  history of, 115–31
  liberation from, 5, 10

  modern discourses on, 6–9, 10, 11, 12. *See also* sexual discourse
  Reich's critique, 131
  See also repressive hypothesis
sexuality
  and alliance systems, 106–13
  and blood relations, 147–9
  of children. *See* children's sexuality
  and class structure, 120–7
  as correlative of discourse, 68–9
  as historical construct, 105–6, 108
  latency principle, 66
  psychoanalysis, role of, 129–30
  relation to sex, 151–7
  as sin, 9
  strategies involving, 103–5
  in Victorian era, 3–4
  See also sex
sin
  confession of, 19–20. *See also* confession
  sexual perversion as, 38
Sixth Commandment, 39
sodomy
  ancient laws, 43
  discourse on, 101
  distinguished from homosexuality, 43
  as sin, 38
  uncertain status, 37
states
  policing of sex, 24–6
  power strategy, 137
suicide, 138–9
Süssmilch, Johann Peter, 140

Tamburini, Tommaso, 19
Tardieu, Auguste, 24, 63
Tartuffe (Molière), 110 n.
Three Essays (Freud), 27
torture, 59 and n.
Tridentine Catholicism, 116
truth
  and confession, 58–63
  pleasure in, 71
Tutor, The (Lenz), 110 n.

About the Author

Michel Foucault was born in Poitiers, France, in 1926. He has lectured in many universities throughout the world and served as Director of the Institut Français in Hamburg and the Institut de Philosophie at the Faculté des Lettres in the University of Clermont-Ferrand. He writes frequently for French newspapers and reviews, and is the holder of a chair at France's most prestigious institution, the Collège de France.

In addition to his classic study, *Madness and Civilization,* M. Foucault is the author of *The Order of Things, The Archaeology of Knowledge, The Birth of the Clinic,* and *I, Pierre Rivière.* His latest book, *Discipline and Punish: The Birth of the Prison,* was published by Pantheon in 1978.